TUCHEL

Tactical

ANALYSIS AND TRAINING ACTIVITIES

CARLOS DOMÍNGUEZ

Tuchel Tactical / Carlos Domínguez - 1st edition
LIBROFUTBOL.com, 2022.

136 pages; 15,2 x 22,9 cm.

ISBN 978-987-8943-48-0

1. Fútbol.
CDD 796.3342

TUCHEL TACTICAL
by Carlos Domínguez

Cover: Luciano Medvetkin Translation: Scott Nelson	Photo of the author: © Carlos Domínguez
© 2022 – Carlos Domínguez © 2022 – LIBROFUTBOL.com	**All rights reserved**
The partial or total reproduction, storage, rental, transmission or transformation of this book, in any form or by any means, electronic or mechanical, by photocopying, digitization or other methods, is not allowed without prior written permission from the publisher. Any violation is punishable by law.	
ISBN 978-987-8943-48-0	1st edition: September 2022

ediciones@librofutbol.com

+54 9 11 2215 1982

librofutbol

Av. del Libertador 6898 - Núñez - City of Buenos Aires - Argentina

INDEX

PROLOGUE

"A team must be hard working, humble, brave, and persistent. Now it's my responsibility to create that environment. How? On the training field, since that is the most important place where we spend time".

That phrase makes a good cover letter. They were his first words upon his arrival at Borussia Dortmund, and they are probably the ones that best describe Thomas Tuchel. He is someone who is meticulous, hard-working, obsessive about tactics, creative, and a great leader. All these traits have catapulted him upwards during his meteoric professional coaching career on the sidelines of some of the best teams in the world, starting as an absolute unknown and reaching the top level after only ten years.

The German is one of the few active coaches who've been able to manage the most sought-after teams in the world without first having had a successful career as a professional player. What was he like as a player? A modest central defender who only played eight games in Bundesliga 2, with Stuttgart Kickers, and finished his sporting career shortly afterwards in the Third Division at Ulm, when a chronic knee injury forced his retirement at just 24 years of age.

He is indeed a very rare breed, and bit by bit we will unravel the ins and outs and the tactical weapons that have made him so successful in such a short time in this complex environment. Only the chosen few ever manage to reach the top level, but Thomas Tuchel is one of the chosen.

STEP 1

Enter Google Play or Apple Store and download the QR Scanning App.

STEP 2

Install and open the App on your mobile phone.

STEP 3

Scan the QR code to access exclusive material.

BEGINNINGS AND CAREER PATH

It's important to start from the beginning and review the trajectory of Thomas Tuchel's coaching career, as well as to take a broad look at his philosophy and playing model. These two important pillars of his coaching are useful if we want to better understand his tactical complexity.

After his short-lived career as a player, a young and restless Tuchel began his coaching career in the youth ranks at Vfb Stuttgart, where he started with the under-14 team and worked his way up to the under-19's. It was during the course of his six years at the club that he met his great mentor and footballing father: Hermann Badstuber.

> *I was very much influenced, both professionally and personally, by Hermann Badstuber. He was a very knowledgeable coach, but at the same time he allowed and encouraged lateral thinking, diligently questioning everything, which allowed him to remain very modest.*

After this initial stage of his career, the Bavarian continued his coaching journey with Augsburg II (2007-2008), moving shortly afterwards to the Mainz 05 under-19's (2008-2009). In this

last cycle he conquered the league, surpassing a star-studded Borussia Dortmund which featured Mario Götze and other prominent names.

And what takes many coaches a lot of time to achieve, if they can achieve it at all, Tuchel managed to do at only 35 years of age. He was offered the opportunity of a lifetime and made his debut among the coaching elite after being in the right place at the right time. At the end of his successful season with the youth team, Mainz 05 gave him the opportunity to sign his first contract coaching a professional team; nothing more and nothing less than the club's first team that had recently been promoted to the Bundesliga, one of the strongest leagues of the world.

With all the charisma and confidence that he is famous for, he accepted the offer and did not disappoint. It was there that he forged an exceptional name and reputation for himself after 182 games and five glorious seasons. He managed to establish the club at the highest level, with financial solvency, and even qualified for the Europa League. Because of his young age and his ability, he become recognized as one of the most promising coaches in Germany.

After this successful spell at Mainz 05, it didn't take long for him to attract the attention of bigger teams, and Borussia Dortmund recruited him for the daunting task of replacing Jürgen Klopp.

In his two years at Dortmund, he achieved several notable records. First, he did not lose any home games in the Bundesliga (recording 27 wins in 34 games), turning the emblematic Signal Iduna Park into a veritable fortress. In addition, his team scored 21 goals in the group stage of the 2016/17 Champions League, which up to that time was the most ever in the history of Europe's top continental competition. Finally, Tuchel said goodbye by lifting the German Cup in 2017 (his first title as coach) after beating Eintracht Frankfurt 2-1. Tuchel closed his cycle at the club with 68 wins, 23 draws, and 17 losses.

These impressive numbers did not go unnoticed, and allowed him to take a bigger and even more dizzying leap in his professional career. The next stop on his career path was the almighty PSG, who envisioned him as the coach who could lead them to their long-awaited first Champions League title.

At this stage of his career he was confronted with a new challenge, unrelated to the purely tactical side of the game: having so many stars together in the same locker room, especially Kylian

Mbappé and Neymar Jr. This was not easy for him to handle and, when combined with Tuchel's own strong character, things didn't end up going so well. there were public spats over substitutions and other issues related to how the German handled things in the changing room.

In a strictly sporting sense, not everything was turbulent. The Parisian side got off to an ideal beginning: marking the best start in Ligue 1 history with a record run of nine wins from their first nine matches. However, from there things got complicated. And so, a club that was built to win absolutely everything was eliminated in the quarterfinals of the League Cup against the modest Guingamp by a score of 2-1, and was eliminated in the quarterfinals of the Champions League by Manchester United. This loss was especially painful as they succumbed to a comeback by the away side after winning 2-0 in the first leg at Old Trafford. In addition, during that season PSG lost the Coupe de France to Stade Rennais in a penalty shootout. The failures of these campaigns were redeemed by the runaway conquest of the league, as PSG finished 16 points ahead of Lille.

Given the disappointing season and the apparent conflicts within the locker room, everything seemed destined for a divorce between the club and the coach. But the board ended the rumors of the split with a vote of confidence in the German, renewing his contract for another year.

The 19/20 season was totally different. Despite experiencing the most difficult year in the history of football due to the pandemic, they experienced a change of fortune in terms of results. Domestically, Tuchel's team won Ligue 1, the League Cup, and the French Cup. In the greatest continental competition, which underwent a change of format with the quarterfinals and semifinals played as single matches in Lisbon, PSG were on the verge of achieving their long-awaited dream of winning their first "big-eared trophy". Tuchel defeated Atalanta in the quarter-finals, overcame his compatriot Julian Nagelsmann's surprising Leipzig in the semi-finals, and lost the final 1-0 to Bayern Munich. Although it was a tough blow, that journey confirmed the Bavarian's status as one of the top coaches on the international scene.

The ghosts of the past reappeared in the following campaign, in which the team's start in Ligue 1 was very irregular. Discrepancies with the board and the sporting director Leonardo over certain planning decisions steered him towards the exit ramp.

Six months after being on the verge of glory in Lisbon, PSG fired Tuchel, who departed a team that had qualified for the round of 16 of the Champions League and was in third place in Ligue 1.

This is how the Bavarian experienced it, as he told Sky Germany: "It was very surprising. I remember it was early in the afternoon on December 22 when I sensed what was going to happen. I had a conversation with the sporting director. I felt that they could fire me, but I didn't think they would. We had just beaten Strasbourg 4-0. We packed up our things in Paris and went home to celebrate Christmas. From a work standpoint, I had a shitty Christmas, but I found the best gift under the tree, and that was Chelsea".

Who could have told Tuchel that just a month after his harsh and unexpected departure from PSG, he would be on the verge of what has been, up to now, his most glorious spell as coach in the beautiful game: his time at Chelsea.

They hired him to replace the club legend Frank Lampard, who did not start the season well with the Blues, who were in ninth place with eight wins, five draws, and six losses. The Bavarian signed for a year and, in a period of six months he changed the English team's image, perfecting an exciting system with five defenders. He was able to soar in the Premier League, achieving a remarkable fourth place finish: the coveted final place that ensures automatic qualification for the Champions League.

He was also runner-up in the FA Cup. After a very good victory in the semifinals over Manchester City, he was one step away from the title but lost at the iconic Wembley Stadium against Leicester City by a score of 1-0.

But the enduring memory of the 20/21 season for Tuchel's Chelsea was the lifting of the Champions League trophy. The team in blue got through the knockout rounds thanks to the execution of his players and the steady efforts of the German coach, who was awarded his doctorate in tactics in front of the eyes of the entire international footballing community.

The road the Londoners took to get there was memorable, with a convincing start against Diego Simeone's Atlético, winning both games (1-0 and 2-0). They then eliminated Porto, with their win in the first leg (2-0) allowing them to advance despite falling in the second leg (1-0). And in the semifinals they beat Zinedine Zidane's Real Madrid during a tie in which they were brilliant in the match in Spain despite not winning (1-1), and sealed their ticket to the final with a clear-cut victory at Stamford Bridge (2-

0). This made Tuchel the first coach in history to coach in two consecutive editions of the final with two different clubs.

So he returned to Portugal a year later with the same goal as before: to become European champions. This time the opponent was Pep Guardiola's Manchester City. As had happened in the previous rounds, the Bavarian managed to impose his tactics and won in the final on that magical night, thanks to a solitary goal from Kai Havertz in the 42nd minute.

Representing both the present and future of top-level international coaching, Thomas Tuchel wrote the most glorious chapter of his biography and reached the peak of the continental game after just six months at Chelsea. This is how he described that conquest: "It is a fantastic achievement. We expected to face a very strong team, and we knew that we were going to have to be at a high level in order to impose ourselves. I'd won at lower levels, but I didn't know what this feeling would be like. Now it's time to celebrate and afterwards we'll go looking for the next success, for the next title."

THOMAS TUCHEL'S USUAL FORMATIONS

1-4-2-3-1

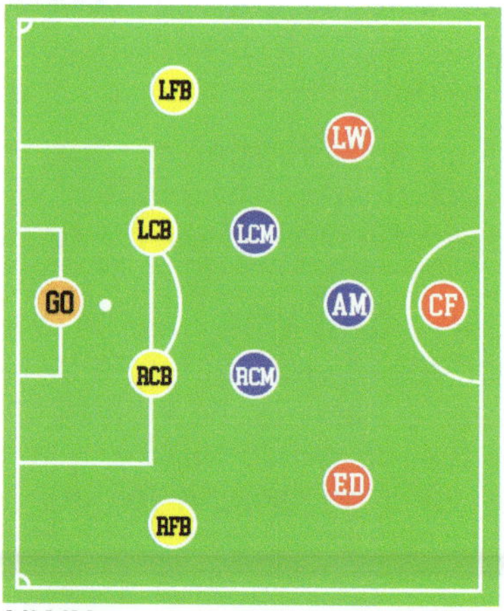

1-3-4-2-1

1-4-1-4-1

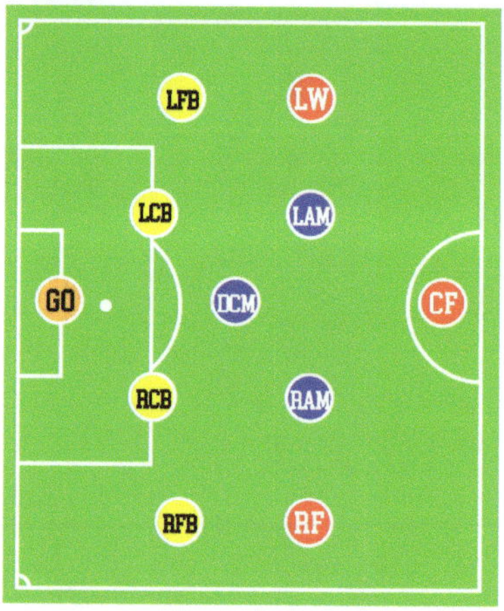

1-4-3-3

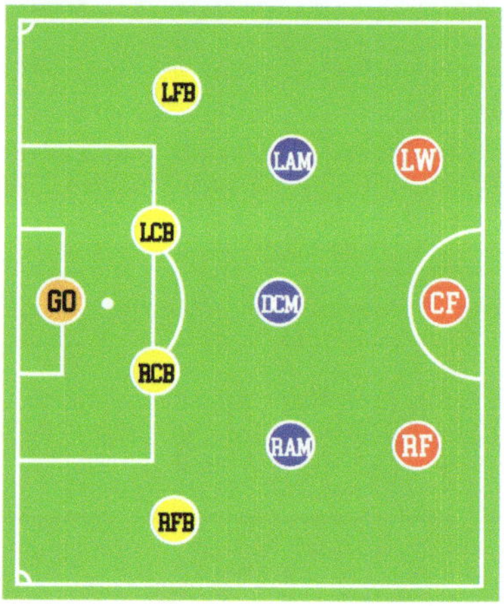

GO GOALKEEPER · **LWB** LEFT WING-BACK · **LCB** LEFT CENTER-BACK · **LFB** LEFT FULLBACK · **CB** CENTER-BACK · **RCB** RIGHT CENTER-BACK

RWB RIGHT WING-BACK · **RFB** RIGHT FULLBACK · **LAM** LEFT ATTACKING MIDFIELDER · **LCM** LEFT CENTER MIDFIELDER · **LCAM** LEFT CENTRAL ATTACKING MIDFIELDER · **DCM** DEFENSIVE CENTER MIDFIELDER

AM ATTACKING MIDFIELDER · **RAM** RIGHT ATTACKING MIDFIELDER · **RCM** RIGHT CENTER MIDFIELDER · **RCAM** RIGHT CENTRAL ATTACKING MIDFIELDER

LW LEFT WINGER · **CF** CENTER FORWARD · **RF** RIGHT FORWARD

SYSTEMS OF PLAY

Now that we've analyzed Tuchel's outstanding career so far, it's time to delve into the tactical part; the evolution of his tactics board. The first conclusion that can be drawn is that we are looking at a very adaptable coach who is not limited to a specific game system. In fact, based on the squad of players at his disposal, he is always varying and modifying how his teams play.

Another point to highlight is his ability to study and analyze his opponents. Each scheme varies according to the rival in front of him: he doesn't leave anything to chance and he doesn't put the system ahead of everything else. That's why his ideal structure always takes into account both his own team and the opponent.

His tactical evolution cannot be understood without chronologically reviewing all the formations he has used in recent years. Although they all retain Tuchel's identity and imprint, they exhibit some important variations in certain phases of the game. So next we will look at the formation that he has used the most.

We must start with 1-4-2-3-1 (Image 1), the first game formation that he developed in his early days as a coach, both at Mainz 05 and at Dortmund. Many times this formation was alternated to a 1-4-1-4-1 (Image 2).

Preserving many aspects of the style of his predecessor Jürgen Klopp, Tuchel managed to impose a style that was more controlled and less vertical, although he did not give up vertical play entirely. One of his strategies was to accumulate a large number of players in the interior channels near the opponent's penalty area and encourage the fullbacks to push up, especially at times when penetrating through the middle wasn't possible.

Image 1

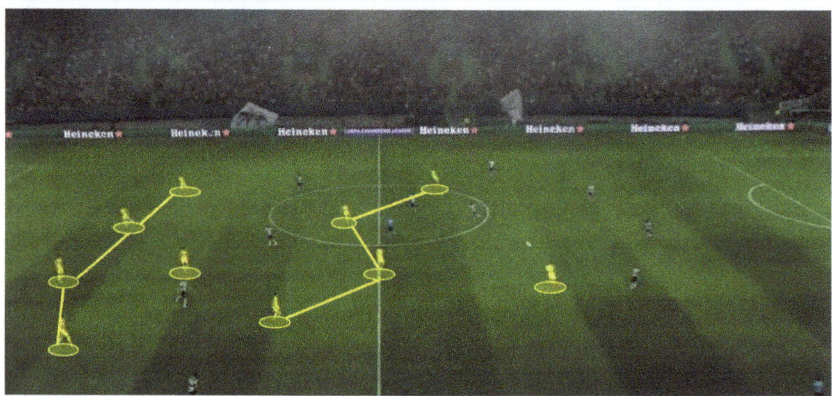

Image 2

Upon his arrival at PSG, Tuchel completely changed his usual system from those previous years. Having vertical players and devastating attacking power at his disposal, he opted for an offensive 1-4-3-3 (Image 3). He also occasionally used other variants, with 1-4-4-2 being the most prominent, although in Paris he made more of an impression with the first option.

That 1-4-3-3 formation was characterized by the freedom in attack enjoyed by Neymar and Mbappé, the two wingers who had a tendency to receive inside in order to create a lot of space on the wings for the advancing fullbacks. The defensive midfielder also played an important role, especially in recovering the ball, allowing the two attacking midfielders to have more freedom in the creation phase.

Image 3

But it's on his most recent stage that the German has found the system that's given him perhaps the most success, and for which he will be most remembered. The model he's created reflects his personality and image, with a distinct identity and some very characteristic patterns. It's a formation that he had used in previous cycles, although not with much continuity. But at Chelsea he found the ideal ecosystem and squad members to develop the 1-3-4-2-1 (Images 4 and 5) that bears his signature.

Thanks to this distribution of players, the team is balanced on both sides of the pitch and maintains a greater stability between the attacking and defending zones. With a line of three powerful centerbacks; some offensive minded wingbacks who are also unselfish and committed to dropping back; a physical midfield with technical qualities; and fast and skillful wingers, Tuchel has managed to put together one of the most consistent teams of recent years. It's a delight to watch and analyze this machine, playing in a fantastic 1-3-4-2-1 system that will undoubtedly continue to be refined over the coming years.

Image 4

Image 5

TUCHEL'S NOTEBOOK

ORGANIZED ATTACK

STARTING PHASE

Basic principles:

Buildout style

Tuchel's teams look to build out from the back, but have also established mechanisms for playing direct if the opponent forces them to do so.

Zones where the buildout starts

They always look to make the first pass inside, which on many occasions allows them to attact pressure and free up space on the outside.

Key players

The centerbacks, the midfielders, the wingbacks, and the goalkeeper.

Level of risk assumed in the starting phase

They assume a moderate level of risk by always trying to build out short, with the participation of the goalkeeper on many occasions.

Height of the outside backs

They position themselves high during the majority of buildout situations.

Mobility in the starting phase

Tuchel's teams are very dynamic and very mobile, especially the midfielders who must provide constant support.

In this first phase of play, the German coach provides his teams with various patterns and rules for building out of the back, which generates lots of options. Tuchel prefers combination play in the buildout, taking some risks and prioritizing short passes. This is the facet of the game to which Tuchel dedicates the most time, and it's not surprising that his central defenders are among the players who make the most passes in the league. His teams try to generate numerical superiority to advance from the back, a superiority Chelsea ensures by using three central defenders (with the two outer centerbacks offering wide support and the central one responsible for starting the process).

In the starting phase we will see the importance of these superiorities that the Bavarian seeks to create whenever his team has the ball. The goalkeeper, centerbacks, midfielders and wingbacks who drop to offer give support provide Chelsea with sufficient numbers and mechanisms to play short out of the back in most situations.

The behavior of the wingbacks is essential, since they play a prominent role in this phase of the game. They do so by receiving the ball via short passes from the centerbacks when there is no way through the central zone, or by offering a long option when playing direct out of the back. These actions usually happen when the opponent plays in a high block.

One of the hallmarks that sets Tuchel's teams apart is the importance of the goalkeeper when it comes to offering additional support and creating superiorities during the buildout, especially when the opponent exerts good pressure. It's common to see the goalkeeper intervene with his feet on numerous occasions, acting as an extra player and a viable alternative in situations in which the centerbacks cannot overcome the opponent's lines of pressure through combination play with nearby teammates.

THE IMPORTANCE OF THE GOALKEEPER

Image 6

In Image 6 we can see Atlético de Madrid pressing three-on-four in a high block. It's in these situations where the importance of using the goalkeeper to create a superiority can be seen most clearly. Acting as an additional player for his team during the buildout, the goalkeeper Édouard Mendy (16) receives the ball from the central defender Kurt Zouma (15), who passes to him due to the impossibility of connecting with the two center midfielders. Mendy has support from the central defenders to minimize the passing risks in the event that possession is lost. In this case, he decides to pass to the left centerback Antonio Rüdiger (2), who now has a clean path to progress in his channel.

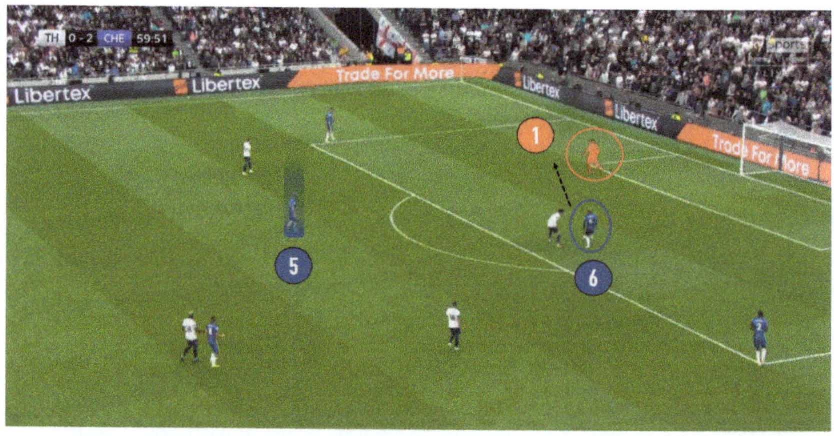

Image 7

In Tuchel's teams, the goalkeeper is just another player in the starting phase who behaves proactively to offer himself as an option, even in situations that are "unnatural" according to how the position is normally conceived. Image 7 shows a clear example in which the goalkeeper Kepa Arrizabalaga (1) moves to provide necessary support to the central defender Thiago Silva (6), who does not have a free passing line to the right midfielder Jorginho (5). In this way, a superiority is achieved despite Tottenham's pressure, and the Spaniard delivers the ball to the open midfielder.

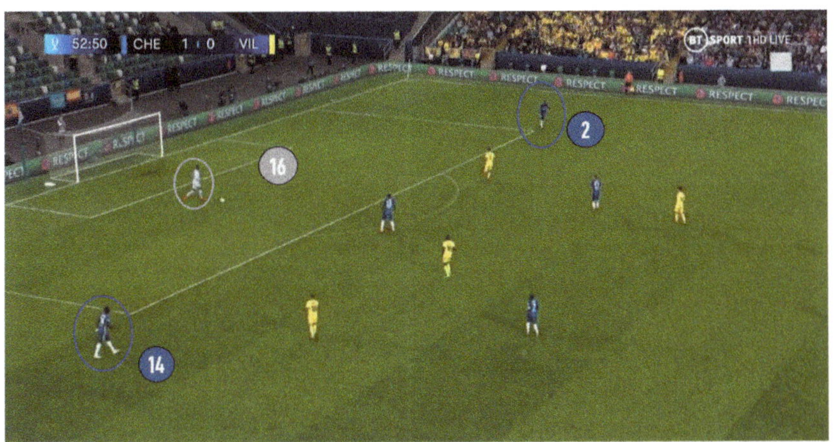

Image 8

In Image 8 we can once again observe the constant support of the outside players in the line of three when the ball is played back to the goalkeeper. When the goalkeeper Édouard Mendy (16) receives the ball, both centerbacks -Trevoh Chalobah (14) on the right and Antonio Rüdiger (2) on the left - immediately move into wide supporting positions, offering themselves as two buildout options to overcome the first line of pressure of Villarreal's high block.

Image 9

In Image 9 we see how the goalkeeper Édouard Mendy (16) cannot pass to either of the centerbacks and decides to go long to the left wingback Marcos Alonso (3), who is almost at the midfield line. Playing direct in the starting phase is an option when faced with high pressure from the opponent.

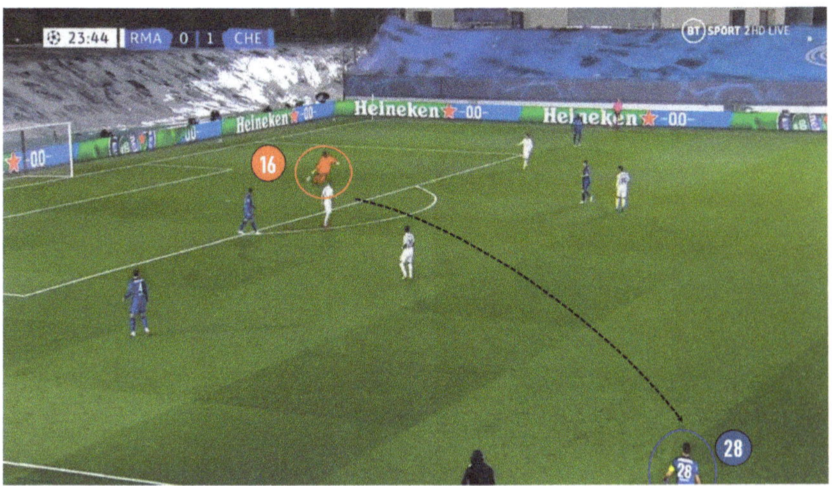

Image 10

This situation is similar to the previous one: Tuchel's team is again subjected to effective pressure from a high block, so the goalkeeper Mendy (16) resorts to playing long to seek out a supporting wingback. In this case it's the right wingback César Azpilicueta (28) who interprets the situation very well and drops down to take up an unmarked position in the interval between the opponent's first and second lines.

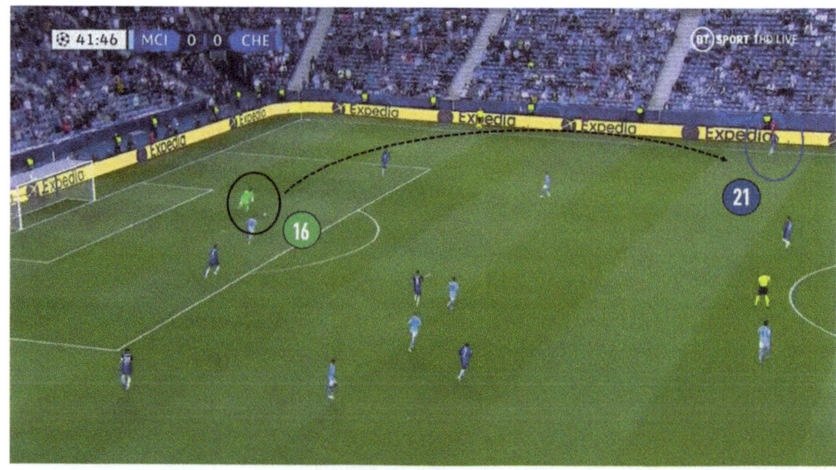

Image 11

This final example of the importance that Tuchel places on goalkeepers during the buildout is surely the most emblematic, from what is probably the most important play of the German coach's career. Image 11 shows the start of the play that led to Chelsea's goal in the Champions League final against Pep Guardiola's Manchester City, which originates in his own penalty area. The goalkeeper Édouard Mendy (16) plays to the left wingback Ben Chilwell (21), who is practically at midfield and receives behind the first line of pressure. This is the key for the subsequent finish by the center forward Kai Havertz.

ATTRACTING THE OPPONENT AND SUPERIORITY THROUGH THE CENTERBACKS

Image 12

In Image 12 we can see one of the buildouts used most frequently by Tuchel's teams. Two fundamental components feature in this phase of the game: the player who occupies the central position in the line of three —the one responsible for making the first decision— and a midfielder who drops down to create a passing line between the attackers who are pressing the back line. We can see how the central player Andreas Christensen (4) is responsible for playing that initial pass and how he connects with the supporting left midfielder Mateo Kovačić (17), who makes himself available behind the back of the opponent's attackers and progresses towards the creation zone after receiving the ball.

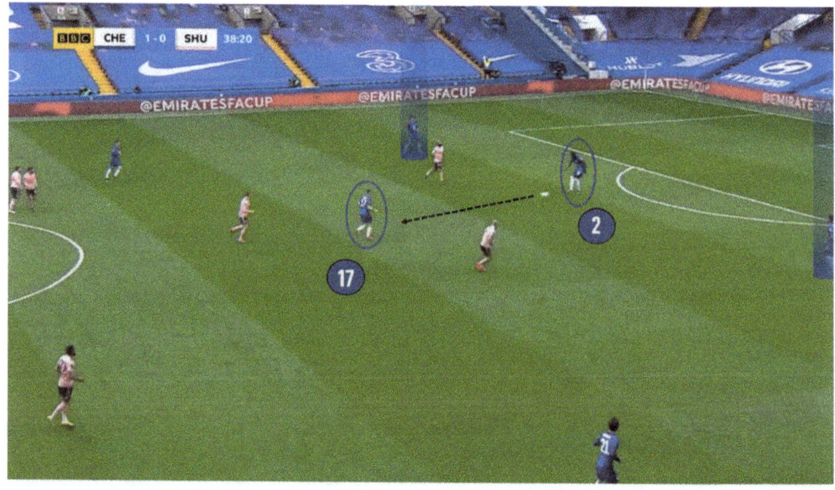

Image 13

Tuchel's buildouts stands out for their variety, since at all times the players have several passing alternatives in the starting phase. For this reason, it's very important that the central defenders, the wingbacks, and the midfielders read the game in order to always have superiority and appropriate support in every situation.

This allows them to fully exploit their most associative version of the buildout. In Image 13 we see how the centerback Antonio Rüdiger (2) plays to the left midfielder Mateo Kovačić (17), who drops down to offer a passing line. Even so, the German also had two other options nearby, thanks to the support out wide from the other two defenders.

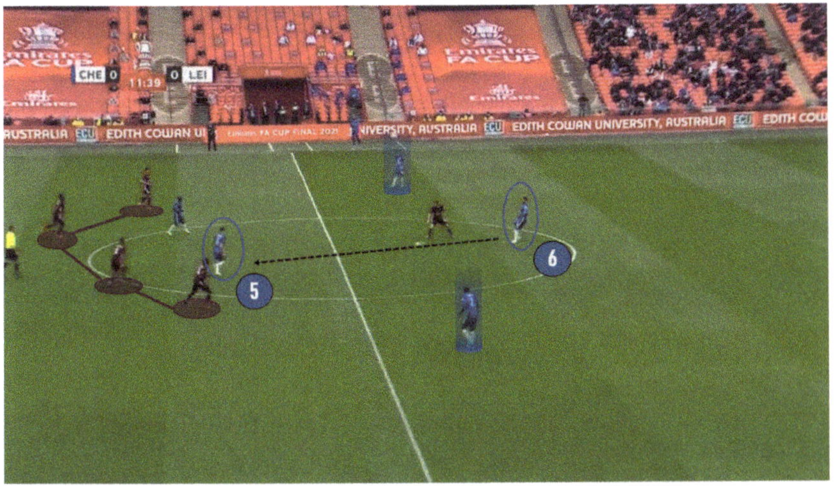

Image 14

The Bavarian coach's teams also face adversaries who defend in a medium block instead of a high block, although this does not excessively modify their mechanisms. As a priority, they maintain the search for the midfielder positioned behind the first line of pressure.

This can also be a method to fix the marking of nearby opponents in order to free up space on the outside, where the wingbacks can advance and the wingers can appear, both between the lines and in the intervals between opponents. In the action shown in Image 14 we see how the left midfielder Jorginho (5) is about to receive the ball and attracts pressure from the opponent, creating a large space where other teammates can appear. The central defender Thiago Silva (6) once again has three options close by as he starts the buildout.

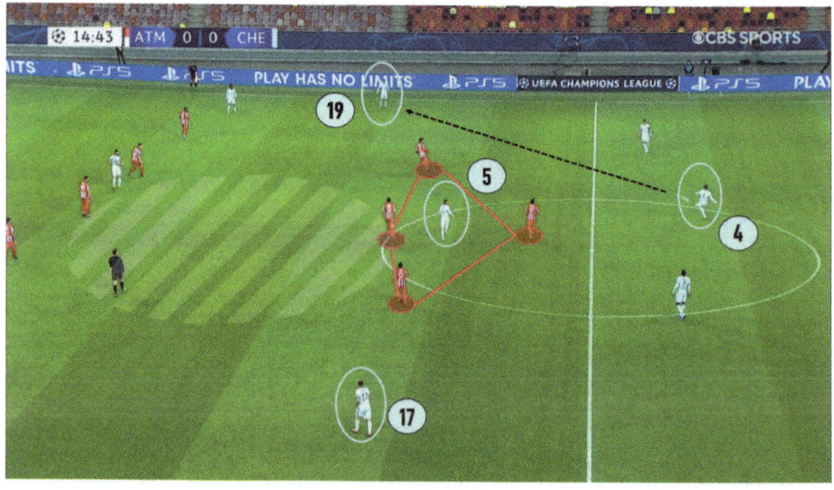

Image 15

Image 15 better reflects those spaces that Tuchel's teams seek to exploit. The right midfielder Jorginho (5) seeks to help the buildout inside, fixing the first line of Atlético de Madrid's defense. This creates a gap behind him that the right winger Mason Mount (19), providing width and offering a clean passing line on the outside, takes advantage of. As always, the player responsible for making that first pass is the centerback, who in this case is Andreas Christensen (4). This also highlights the mobility of the left midfielder Mateo Kovačić (17), who does not show as a short option, but instead is on the move to create free space or provide support higher up the field.

HEIGHT OF THE WINGBACKS

So far we have seen some examples of how Tuchel's teams play long to the wingbacks when no short outlet is available. But these players are also important assets for progressing via short passes.

Image 16

As previously mentioned, the wingbacks in Tuchel's teams are initially placed in advanced positions, on many occasions almost at the midfield line. But the Bavarian coach knows how to give his players the tools to develop an extraordinary ability to read each phase of the game. That is why the players who occupy these positions understand perfectly when to move up and when to move down the field.

An example can be seen in Image 16, in which the left wingback Marcos Alonso (3) reads the situation and drops down from his position to support the left center back Antonio Rüdiger (2), who faces pressure from the high block.

Image 17

This is a recurring solution that is used against teams who defend in a middle block. In this case we see an action in which the central zone of the field is very well covered by the opponent's first line of defense, making the usual pass between a centerback and a center midfielder impossible. That's why the right back Reece James (24) adjusts his position and moves to provide an outlet on the outside where he can receive the ball from the right centerback César Azpilicueta (28).

CENTER MIDFIELDER SUPPORTING A WINGBACK

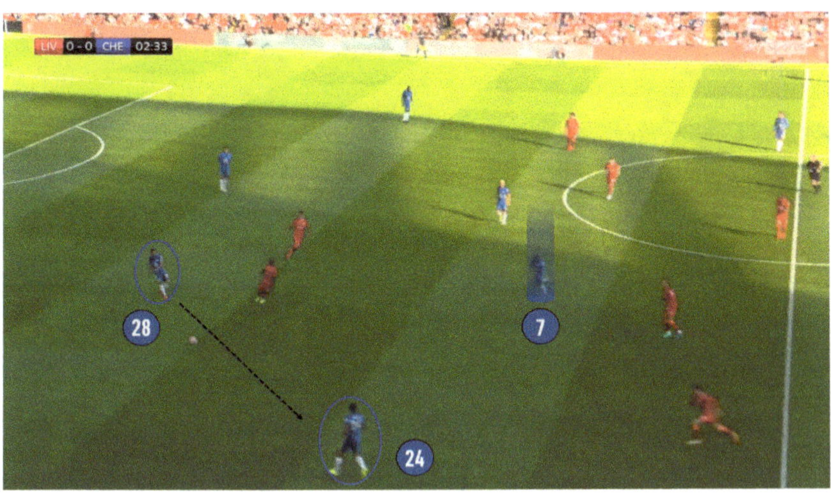

Image 18

An important component of the offensive structure of Tuchel's teams lies in the dynamism and mobility of his center midfielders, who provide continual support in the outer zones during the starting phase. Image 18 shows another buildout with a pass from the right centerback Cesar Azpilicueta (28) to the right wingback Reece James (24), who appears to provide a short option. Upon receiving the ball, the Englishman has a passing line to the right midfielder N'Golo Kanté (7), who slides towards that wing to offer support. This movement is important for the creation of the superiorities that the German coach's teams are looking for in all of their phases with the ball.

Image 19

In Image 19 we find the same three protagonists as in the previous example, but from a different match. The right centerback Azpilicueta (28) plays to the wing for the right wingback James (24), while the right center midfielder Kanté (7) rushes over to support. in this action, the reaction of the opponent prompts the Englishman to play back to the Spaniard.

CREATION PHASE

Basic principles:

Style of play in the creation phase

Mixed. In this phase of the game, one begins to see more actions in which Tuchel's teams seek to play more direct and vertical.

Zones where the creation phase is carried out

The midfielders look to the exterior zones, achieving superiorities with the wingers and the wingbacks out wide.

Key players.

The wingbacks, the center midfielders, and the wingers.

Mobility in the creation phase

These teams are very dynamic in the creation phase. They tend to switch play a lot, which requires constant movement.

Progression through the centerbacks

This is a recurring feature of Tuchel's teams, with one of the centerbacks running with the ball to overcome the opponents' lines of pressure.

Leaving three players back in the creation phase

The German coach's teams use many players in the offensive phase, but always leave three players back for protection. These can be three centerbacks, or a center midfielder can help perform this function. All the other players actively participate in the attack.

The behavior of Tuchel's teams in the creation phase usually varies according to the opponent, the defensive system they are facing, and the moment of the match. This is an extension of the buildout, a stage in which they are generally in less of a hurry. But unlike the buildout, in this second phase of their offensive strategy they try to impose greater speed and verticality on their game. The teams led by the Bavarian coach have mechanisms for adopting a direct style, with situations in which the outside backs and wingers seek to make runs behind the opposing defense. The center forward always tries to stretch the field, fixing the centerbacks so that his teammates can appear in the spaces that are created.

As we have seen in the basic principles, the German coach provides his team with the resources needed to develop both a vertical and an associative playing style. This second variant stands out for the continuous switches of play carried out by the center midfielders to the outside zones, where the wingbacks and wingers play a fundamental role in creating superiorities on the flanks in order to reach the finishing zone as soon as possible. These situations are generated when the opponent defends in a medium or low block.

Another pattern uses the centerbacks to run with the ball to break the first line of pressure, often taking advantage of the numerical advantages generated from behind and the confusion that occurs when the opponent must step up.

DIRECT PLAY TO THE WINGBACKS

Image 20

One of the main variants of this direct play towards the wings is to look for the wingbacks in a relatively uncomplicated situation. In Image 20 we see how the centerback Christensen (4) launches a long ball directly against Porto's advanced back line. His delivery is aimed at the right wingback James (24), who finds a two-on-one superiority out wide thanks to the supporting winger.

Image 21

Such is the freedom of these players in the offensive phase that they have even generated this unusual option: a long pass from a central defender to a wingback behind the rival's back line. By playing the ball deep, this movement can be converted directly into a finishing action. In Image 21 we can see how the left wingback Marcos Alonso (3) appears from the second line and dismarks behind the opponent's back line, who appear to be be caught by surprise. The defender responsible for the buildout, in this case Thiago Silva (6), is always paying attention to the movements ahead of him and looking for an advantage for his team.

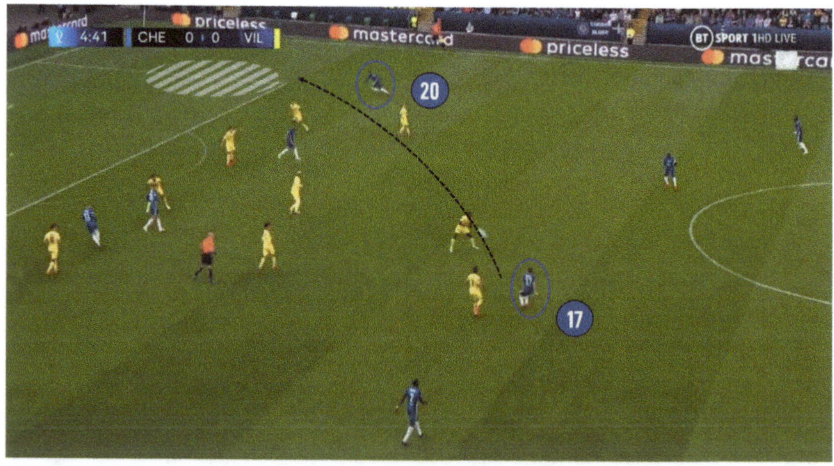

Image 22

This option is even used against teams defending in a low block, as shown in Image 22. The midfielders are the ones who dictate play during these situations in the creation phase, and they are always attentive to wide players who are looking to dismark. In this action, the most important player for Tuchel at that moment of the game is the player responsible for delivering that long pass: the left midfielder Mateo Kovačić (17). The wingback initiating the movement on the right side is Callum Hudson-Odoi (20).

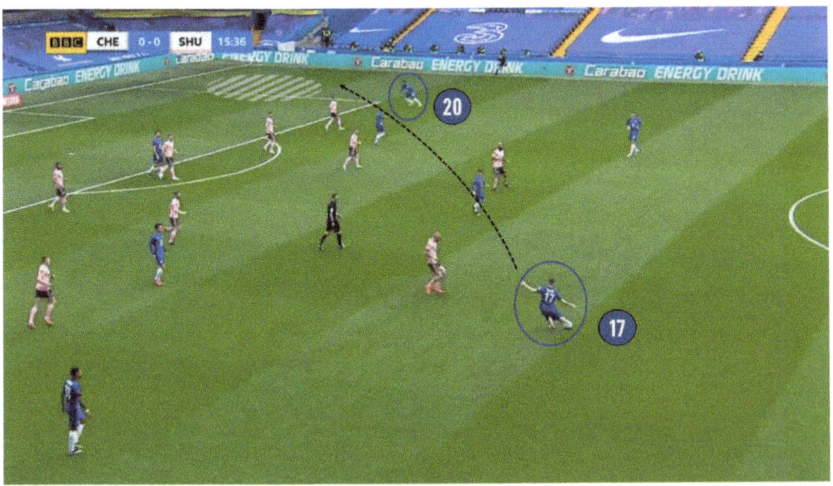

Image 23

In Image 23 we can see a repetition of the previous move. The opponent is defending in a low block and the same protagonists are involved. The right wingback Hudson-Odoi (20) dismarks behind the defense and the left midfielder Kovačić (17) plays another magnificent long pass.

CENTERBACK RUNNING WITH THE BALL

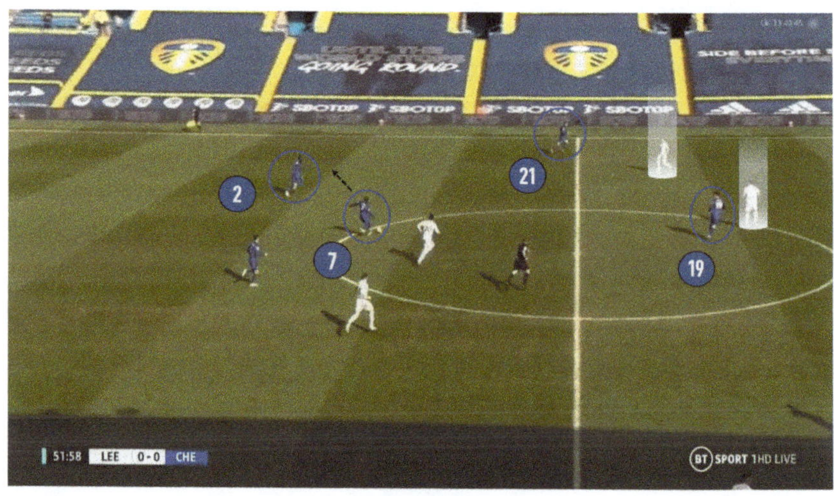

Image 24

Another noticeable pattern in Tuchel's teams is the freedom that the central defenders have to progress with the ball and break lines in situations that are conducive to it. Image 24 shows a pass from the right midfielder N'Golo Kanté (7) to the left centerback Antonio Rüdiger (2), in an action that sometimes creates confusion for opposing defenses. We can see how Marcelo Bielsa's Leeds United are pressing with two strikers and Chelsea have a superiority as they build out of the back with the ball. The Argentine's squad are keeping watch on their opponents and are ready to cover potential passes to the left wingback Ben Chilwell (21) and the attacking midfielder Mason Mount (19), who move to provide close-range support.

Image 25

This situation means that Rüdiger (2) can advance several meters with the ball without any opposition, thanks to the fact that his teammates are fixing the Leeds United markers. Since no opponent steps up, the German enters the opposing half of the field and looks to play the ball into space for Chilwell (21) from a very advanced position, as can be seen in Image 25.

Image 26

Here is another clear example of the freedom that the centerbacks have in this type of situation. By simply running with the ball, they are able to reach advanced areas of the field to finish the play. In Image 26, the right midfielder Jorginho (5) finds the free man; the left centerback Antonio Rüdiger (2).

Image 27

As shown in Image 27, Rüdiger (2) has run with the ball from box to box. Among all of Tuchel's players, the German is surely one of the best equipped to carry out this type of action, due to his powerful running and his good ball handling skills.

As he reaches the attacking third of the field, the centerback running with the ball has three passing options to finish the play, as seen in Image 27. At the same time, those teammates have made it easier for him to maneuver by fixing their opponents.

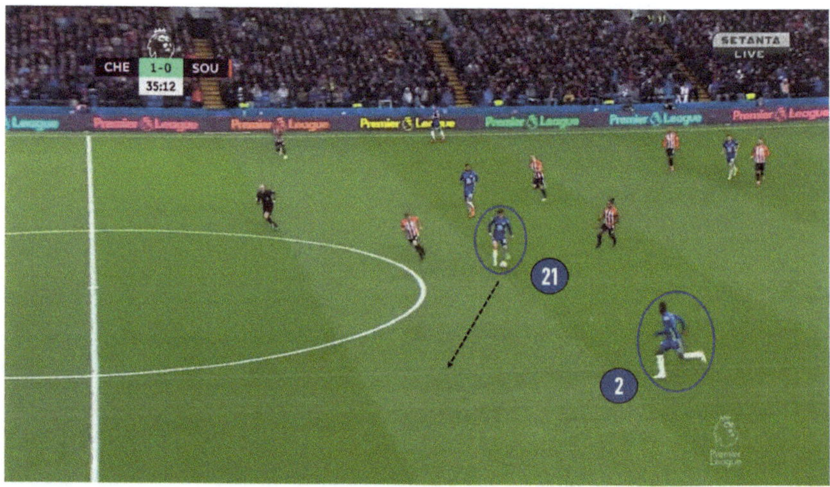

Image 28

There's no better example than this action to demonstrate this pattern of play. With three simple passes, Tuchel's team is able to go from a throw-in in their own half, which Southampton presses in a high block, to playing at devilish speed and taking advantage of the incorporation of a free defender. Again, the protagonist is the left centerback Rüdiger (2), who receives the ball in midfield from the left back Ben Chilwell (21) after a quick switch of play. (Which is an important aspect of the creation phase, as we will see).

Image 29

Rüdiger (2) shows his ability to cover ground with the ball, dribbling past the only opposing defender in his path and arriving at the edge of the penalty area. There, as we can see in Image 29, he is able to thread the ball into space for the center forward Romelu Lukaku (9), who converts the chance with a great finish. This action is a reflection of the verticality that characterizes Thomas Tuchel's teams, and is a good example of how each team member is required to read the game and interpret their role, something that the German coach knows how to instill in his players.

SWITCHING PLAY

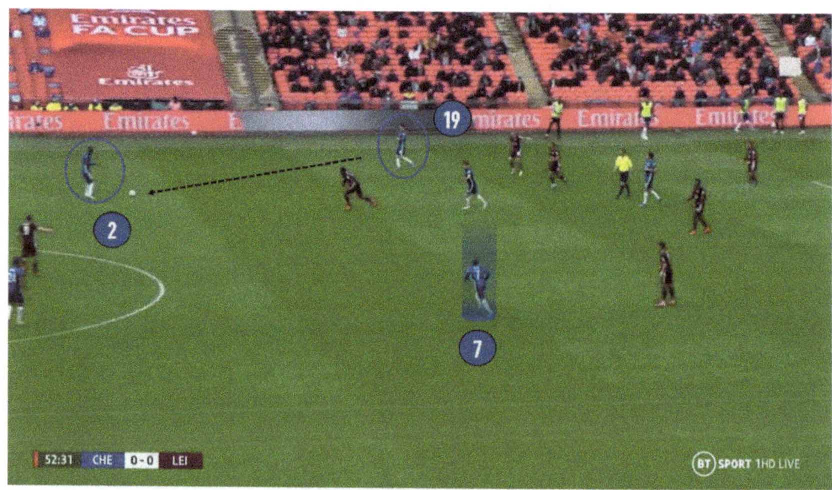

Image 30

Against defenses that organize in a medium or low block, It's clear that Tuchel's teams look to play on the wings, putting a lot of players in those areas and looking for superiorities there that will allow them to progress and finish. To do this, he infuses speed into his teams' attacks, and if they can't find the right situation on one side, they don't hesitate to quickly move the ball to the other side. This requires dynamism and mobility from all the attacking players involved in the creation phase.

In the sequence that begins in Image 30 we see the importance of switches of play, which happen continuously when the Bavarian coach's teams play against opponents who have well organized defensive systems and can close off the outside zones. On this occasion it's the left winger Mason Mount (19) who decides to play the ball back to the left central defender Antonio Rüdiger (2), due to the team's inability to combine down that wing. Immediately, one of the midfielders is activated to provide support for the switch the play. The right midfielder N'Golo Kanté (7) is the player who acts as an outlet to help the German defender move the ball quickly to the other side of the field.

Image 31

In Image 31 we can see how six of the opposing players from Leicester are forced to quickly shift to the other side. Through continuous swtiches of play, Tuchel's teams are looking to create imbalances and disorganize the opponent's defensive block and find superiorities on the opposite wing that will help them penetrate. As the action continues, Kanté (7) plays to the right wingback César Azpilicueta (28), who is positioned out wide.

Image 32

There are many matches in which the German coach's teams face opponents who decide to defend in a low block. These scenarios force them to use constant switches of play as a regular strategy, looking for the smallest detail that they can exploit in order to penetrate into the finishing zone. In Image 32, the right centerback Cesar Azpilicueta (28) decides to play back to the left midfielder Jorginho (5), who is supporting from behind.

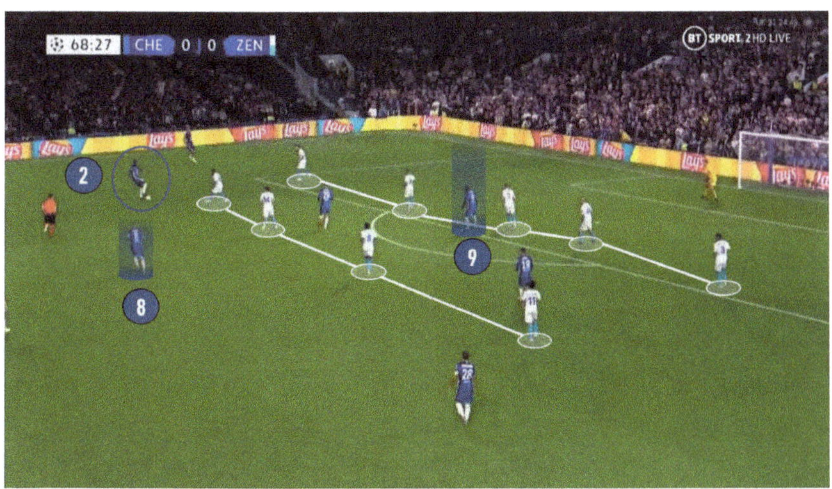

Image 33

Tuchel's team switches the direction of play completely to the other side of the field, in search of a superiority that does not appear at this time, due to the good defensive work of an opponent who are defending with nine players plus the goalkeeper at the edge of their own penalty area. In Image 33 we can see how the left centerback Antonio Rüdiger (2) again passes to a midfielder who has come to support, in this case the right midfielder Mateo Kovačić (8), who again looks to switch the direction of play. In these situations the center forward Romelu Lukaku (9) has a very important role, which is to fix the opposing centerbacks. He also serves as an option when Tuchel's players are unable to find the right ecosystem for an attack on the outside.

Image 34

Another switch of play produces one of those small imbalances that seem insignificant but that do not go unnoticed by Thomas Tuchel's teams, who know how to take advantage of them. In Image 32 the defender charged with covering Lukaku (9) is perfectly positioned behind him, controlling him at all times. But a short time later, after the second movement of the ball in Image 34, we see that Chelsea forces that small mistake in the marking, and the opposing centerback loses track of the Belgian for a few seconds when he must change his body orientation to the other side. César Azpilicueta (28) does not hesitate and puts in a magnificent cross for Lukaku (9), who converts the chance with a great header.

It's an example of how much the smallest details matter, and how the German coach understands them and seeks to exploit them.

SUPERIORITIES AND TRIANGLES ON THE WINGS

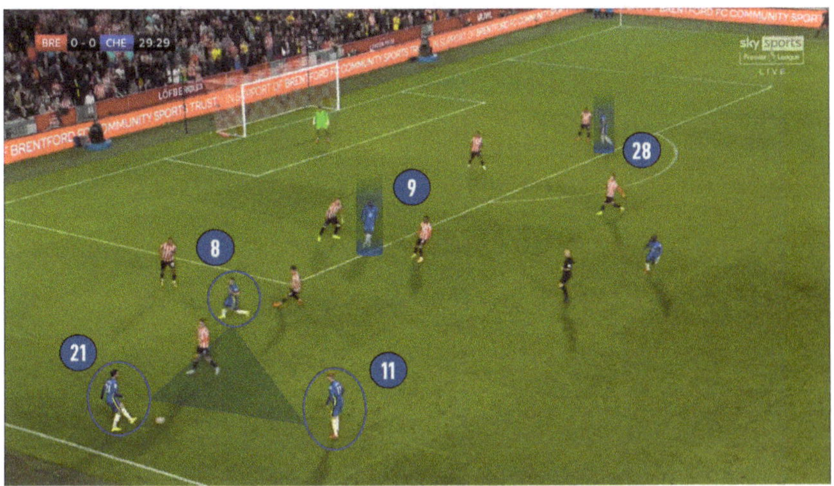

Image 35

The perfect ecosystem forTuchel's teams to overcome organized defenses in a medium or low block includes other aspects and particularities. One important aspect is in their positioning and how they try to find superiorities on the outside through triangular structures and the fixing of opponents farther away by the center forward and the opposite-sided wingback.

In Image 35 we can clearly see this distribution of players, with a concept of forming triangles that is very elaborate and attempts to generate and exploit an advantage on the outside. In these actions, the freedom of roles is very noticeable and the variations available to the participating players are limiteless. Midfielders, wingers, and wingbacks will distribute themselves perfectly as the player in possession, the supporting player, and the reference point, as in this play where the left wingback Ben Chilwell (21), right forward Timo Werner (11), and left attacking midfielder Mateo Kovačić (8)fulfill these three functions, respectively.

Additionally, in the opposing penalty area there is an indirect collaboration with the center forward Romelu Lukaku (9) and the right wingback César Azpilicueta (28). These two players are responsible for fixing defenders and freeing up space, and are also ready to appear in the finishing phase.

Image 36

Image 36 shows the same setup, but with a variation in the configuration of players that make up the triangle: the left wingback Marcos Alonso (3), left winger Mason Mount (19), and right winger Kai Havertz (29). This exemplifies the freedom of movement that the wingers are allowed during the creation phase. In this case, we can see the space that is generated between Havertz (29), the reference point of the triangle, and the center forward Romelu Lukaku (9), who is responsible for fixing the central defenders and can eventually act as the finisher in these situations. Once again, the right wingback Reece James (24) is high up the field to look for a shooting opportunity or to be ready for a possible switch of play.

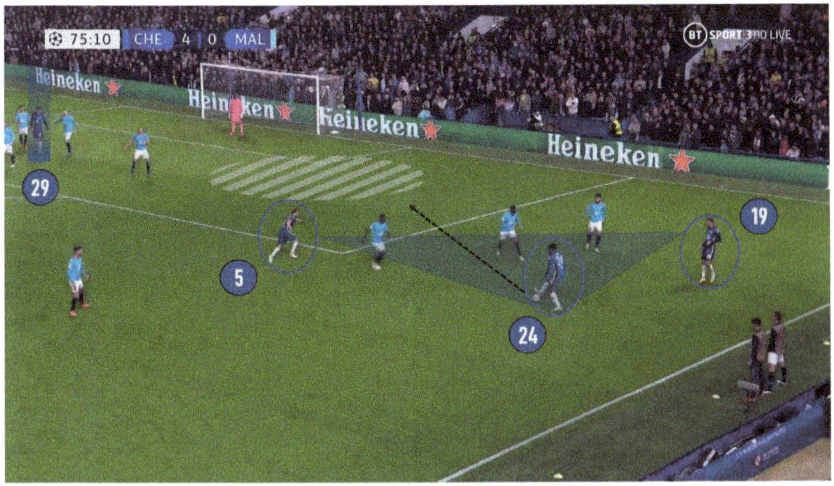

Image 37

This triangular structure with the fixing of distant opponents can allow one of the three protagonists to dismark and penetrate. In the sequence shown in Image 37 the right midfielder Jorginho (5), with his excellent reading of the game, attacks the empty space and receives the ball from the right wingback Reece James (24), who interprets the situation well and plays the pass into space. Next to him, the right winger Mason Mount (19) offers support to complete the shape. Inside the penalty area, the center forward Kai Havertz (19) fixes the centerbacks and is actively waiting for a scoring opportunity in the finishing phase.

FINSIHING PHASE

Basic Principles:

Finishing style

In the vast majority of cases, finishing is through crosses or passes cut back from the end line. Less frequently, finishing is through medium- and long-range shooting.

Zones where the finishing phase is carried out

In the wide zones, thanks to the height of the wingbacks.

Key players

The wingbacks, the wingers, and the center forward.

Mobility in the finishing phase

The wingers, wingbacks, and forwards who participate in these actions all demonstrate a great degree of mobility and look to generate space, dismark behind opponents, and make diagonal runs.

Players who reach the finishing zone

Tuchel's teams usually reach the finishing zone with plenty of players: the two wingbacks, the center forward, at least one winger, and almost always one of the midfielders looking to intercept a clearance.

The German coach's teams are characterized by finishing plays with crosses and passes that are cut back from the wings, taking advantage of their superiorities and wingbacks who reach the end line. This is their comfort zone, and that's why a very high percentage of their organized attacks are concluded in this way.

As in the previous phases, the wingbacks are very important. In this system, their physical deployment is essential and they can join the attack freely. In most of these actions, one of them is responsible for delivering the ball into the area while the other looks for a finishing opportunity at the far post, acting as another striker. In fact, these players are regular goal scorers in Tuchel's teams.

The center forward always attacks the area near the penalty spot when his teammates cross the ball, in search of finishing opportunities or to free up space for a teammate to exploit by dragging the centerbacks. In this phase, the wingers are allowed a lot of freedom of movement and must read the game very well, an ability instilled in them by their German coach. Normally, one of the two wingers is always in the penalty area, looking for finishing opportunities. The other winger can also enter the area or read which spaces he thinks will be more interesting to occupy, for example taking up a position at the top of the penalty area in anticipation of a possible clearance.

The midfielders have more of a secondary role, but they also have the freedom to participate in the finishing phase. They usually do so through medium or long distance shooting and, on many occasions, by being on the alert for possible clearances.

In addition, Tuchel is a coach who employs center forwards with different profiles according to the game plan and the characteristics of his opponent. Sometimes he plays with more of a target player, such as Romelu Lukaku, and at other times he uses a more mobile forward such as Kai Havertz. Nevertheless, once they are in the finishing zone their positioning and function remain very similar.

MAIN STRUCTURE

Image 38

Image 38 reflects two of the most important concepts for Tuchel's teams in terms of their finishing positions. One is the height of the wingbacks, with Callum Hudson-Odoi (20) having the complete freedom to reach the end line and put in the cross. The other, as the center forward, always attacks the area around the penalty spot, knowing that on many occasions the crosses will reach this location. In this case, Timo Werner (11) attacks that area as his teammate prepares to cross, getting behind the opposing center back. Likewise, you can also see the initial disposition of those who arrive from the second line, occupying the spaces in a uniform and rational manner.

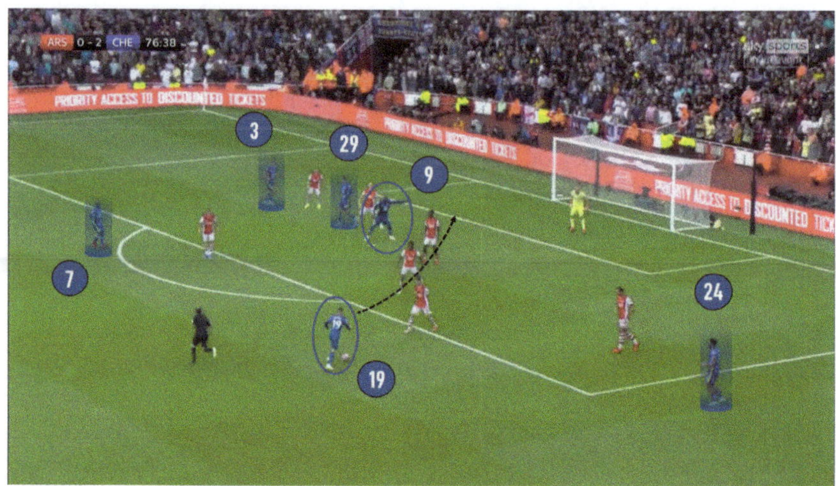

Image 39

In Image 39 we can see a clear example of the distribution of players in the finishing spaces. The center forward Romelu Lukaku (9) is positioned at the penalty spot, trying to beat the center back and demanding a cross into this area. The player responsible for crossing the ball is the right winger Mason Mount (19), who is open after receiving the ball from Reece James (24), the wingback positioned out wide.

We can see how the left winger Kai Havertz (29) and the left wingback Marcos Alonso (3) - who always arrives at the far post - appear to be well distributed in the finishing zone. Finally, you can see how the left midfielder N'Golo Kanté (7) positions himself in the zone in front of the penalty area to pounce on any possible clearance.

Image 40

The center forward is not only important for finishing off crosses; he is also useful for fixing the centerbacks. In the action shown in Image 40, Romelu Lukaku (9) embeds himself near the goalkeeper's box in order to free up space.

Players who advance from behind, especially the wingers, know how to interpret these actions very well and how to appear in the finishing zones, whether on the inside or the outside. In this example, the left winger Kai Havertz (29) is the player who arrives unmarked and occupies that free space. The left wingback Marcos Alonso (3) observes this dismarking and centers the ball towards that area.

In addition, in Image 40 we see how several players appear at the edge of the penalty area, either to support the wingback as the left midfielder Mateo Kovačić (8) does, or to try to control a potential second ball as the right midfielder Jorginho (5) looks to do. Finally, another aspect to highlight is how the right wingback César Azpilicueta (28) enters the penalty area from the opposite side to join the finishing zone.

WINGBACKS AS ADDITIONAL FORWARDS

Image 41

Wingbacks are among the most important players in Tuchel's teams and they play an important role in the finishing zone, with distinctive and interesting behaviors. Surely, this is the position that demands the most physically from the components that make up the German's teams.

During organized attacks, the wingbacks are always required to advance into the opponent's penalty area and appear in the finishing zone. The objective is to force the opposing defense to pay close attention to them throughout the match.

In Image 41 we see a clear example of how one of these players constantly remains in a finishing position. When the attacking midfielder Hakim Ziyech (22) crosses the ball, only the center forward and the left wingback Ben Chilwell (21) are in the penalty area. The Moroccan sees the dismarking of the Englishman and looks to deliver the ball behind the marking defender's back.

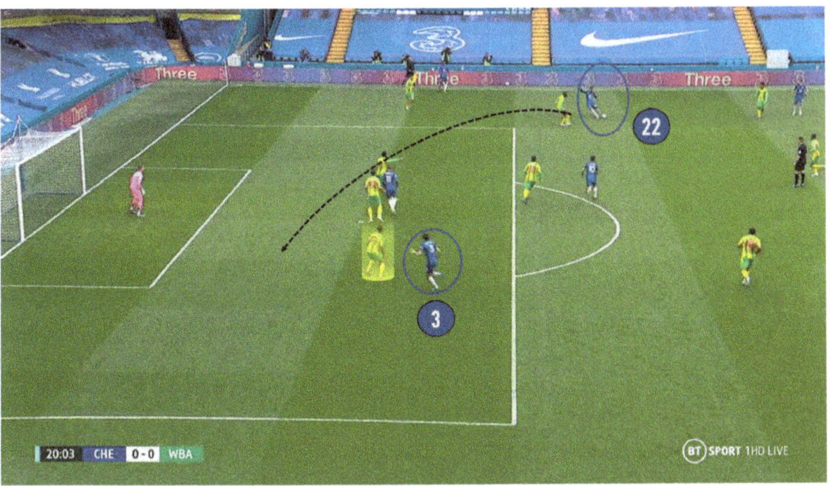

Image 42

In Image 42 we can see how the wingback arrives in a shooting area naturally, as if he were a striker. On this occasion it's Marcos Alonso (3) on the left side who dismarks behind his defender while anticipating the cross from the right winger Hakim Ziyech (22), who reads the situation perfectly.

Image 43

The play in Image 43 is very similar, with the left wingback Ben Chilwell (21) arriving in the penalty area. From the weak side, the Englishman gets behind his defender and attacks the area at the far post in order to finish off a precise cross from the right winger Mason Mount (19).

CLEARANCE ZONE

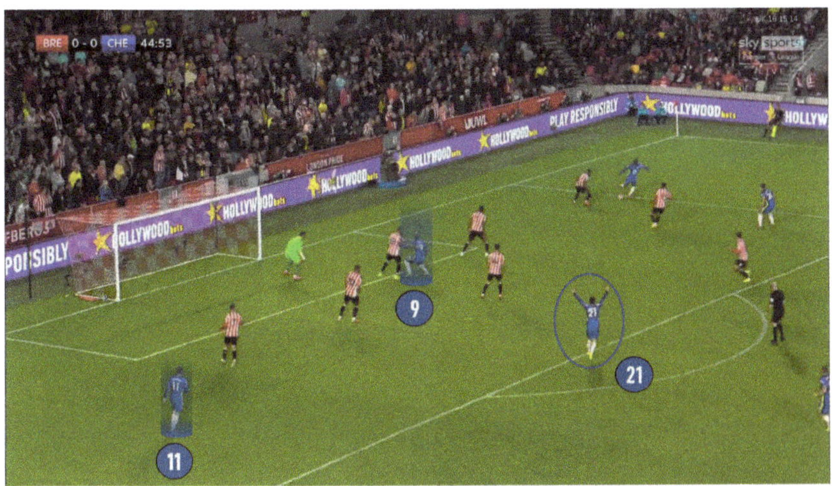

Image 44

With their positioning in the finishing zone, Tuchel's teams also manage the clearance zones. In the vast majority of their attacks there is at least one player at the edge of the penalty area, which allows them to take advantage of any second ball that results from the crosses they look to deliver.

In Image 44 we see a positional exchange between the wingback and the left winger, a situation that occurs on many occasions and demonstrates the players' excellent positional sense and ability to interpret space. The left forward Timo Werner (11) occupies the area at the far post, which generally belongs to the wingback. On this occasion, that wingback Ben Chilwell (21) takes advantage of this development and moves to find free space at the edge of the penalty area.

While this is happening, it's also a good opportunity to analyze the positioning of the center forward Romelu Lukaku (9), who is fixing the defense and will get on the end of the cross. In the continuation of the action, Chilwell (21) wins the second ball and coverts the scoring chance with a great shot.

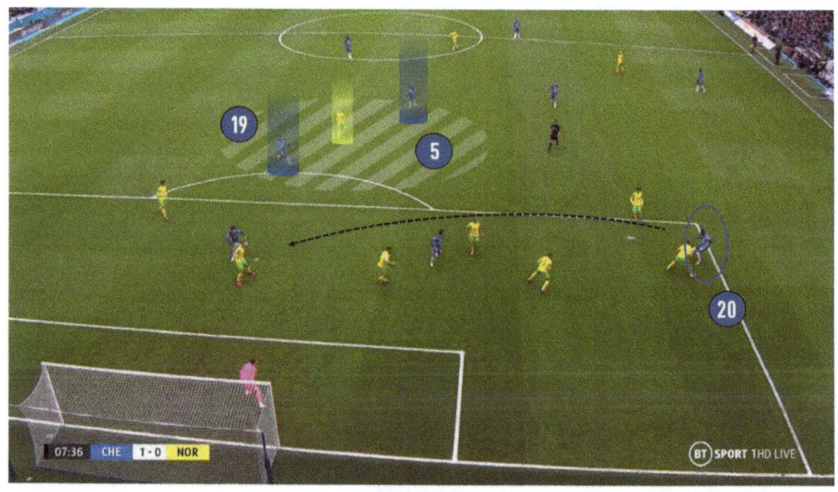

Image 45

This perspective from Image 45 helps us better understand why Tuchel stresses the importance of second balls to his players. His teams tend to dominate these actions, which contribute to their victories in many matches. We can see how the left winger Callum Hudson-Odoi (20) crosses the ball into the heart of the penalty area.

The right winger Mason Mount (19) is situated in free space at the top of the box. In addition, the right midfielder Jorginho (5) has joined from the second line, and there are now two attackers facing just one opponent. This gives them a numerical superiority if the ball is cleared to this zone.

Image 46

Once that ball drops at the edge of the penalty area (Image 46), Tuchel's team acts decisively and takes advantage of their accumulation of players to win the second ball. In this case the ball falls to Jorginho (5) who, perfectly positioned, exploits their superiority and connects with Mason Mount (19) to leave the opponent behind. Unmarked, the Englishman can simply turn towards the goal and covert the opportunity.

OFFENSIVE TRANSITION

Basic Principles:

Behavior of the team after recovering the ball in a lower block

When facing teams that don't press or who defend in a low block, Tuchel's teams will generally play patiently if they must, but will look to punish their opponents with quick transitions when they can.

Where the transitions are carried out

Unlike their organized attacks, in which they generally look to play out wide, in transition they tend to strike more through the inside channels.

Behavior of the team after recovering the ball in a higher block

In these situations, Tuchel's teams are usually in a middle block and with sufficient players in offensive zones when they recover the ball. That is why they generally don't look to go forward quickly and instead seek to develop the play more.

Where the transitions are carried out

Here, Tuchel's teams tend to use the outer channels more, looking for the wingbacks and wingers via switches of play.

Key players

The wingbacks, the wingers, and the center forward.

Tuchel is a genuine artist when it comes to offensive transitions. From his beginnings at Mainz 05 and throughout his career as a coach, he has been perfecting one of the most beautiful and aesthetically pleasing phases of the game. Within the different squads that he has managed, he has been able to find players with an ideal profile to achieve a dynamic style of play, from Marco Reus at Borussia Dortmund to Neymar and Kylian Mbappé at Paris Saint-Germain.

The German coach has always managed to make an impression with clean, vertical, and fast transitions. He knows how to teach his squads to interpret what speed of play is needed at any moment, and you can clearly see that his players understand what individual roles they must assume whenever they recover the ball. Their behavior changes depending on the area of the field in which the recovery occurs, as we will analyze below.

It's assumed that Tuchel's teams will be superior to and dominate their opponents in many games, and that they will usually face opponents who defend in a low block and leave few players up high to attack. The vast majority of time when faced with this type of opponent, the Bavarian's teams typically choose to keep the ball and organize their buildout structure in order to calmly develop their offensive phase. However, against teams who play in the opposite way and leave a lot of space behind them when they lose the ball, Tuchel's focus shifts to damaging the opponent through his two wingers and the center forward, who quickly attack those gaps while playing with a minimal amount of touches.

Things change notably when the German's teams transition from an area higher up the field, as they will take a little pause and look for a structure similar to the one used in their organized attacks. Here, the wingbacks and changes of direction reappear to try to take advantage of superiorities on the outside of the field

TRANSITION FROM A LOWER BLOCK

Image 47

In this first situation (Image 47), Tuchel's team recovers the ball in their own half and chooses to play patiently and organize their structure before starting an organized attack. When the right winger Mason Mount (19) wins the ball, he leaves it for the left midfielder Jorginho, who looks forward and sees that there is only one teammate matched up against the opponent's entire defensive line, which has dropped deep. This is an ecosystem that is not conducive to the kind of transitions that the German's teams feel most comfortable with.

Image 48

That is why Tuchel's team chooses to organize itself and triangulate between the wingbacks, the centerbacks, and the midfielders in order to build the play from the back. In this way, they give pause to the game instead of launching a counterattack into a situation where there is no advantage. It's a reflection of the lessons that the Bavarian coach teaches his players in terms of reading of the game. In Image 48 we see how the ball ends up with the goalkeeper Édouard Mendy (16), who only begins the team's organized advance once the players are perfectly positioned.

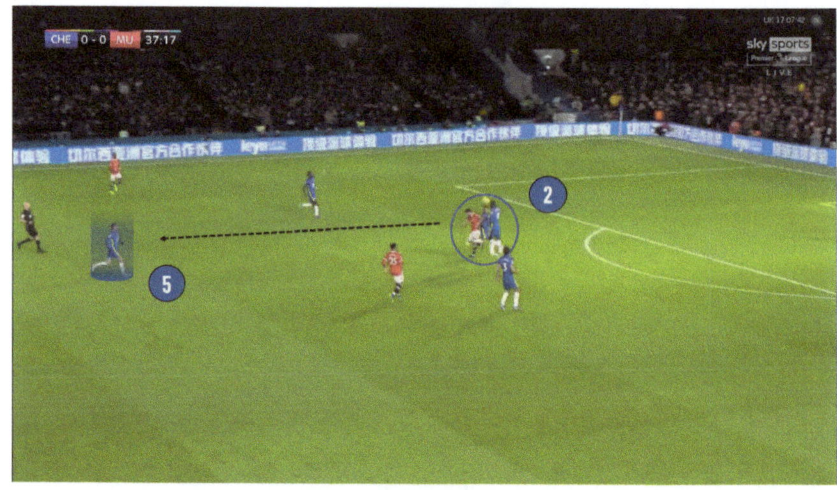

Image 49

Another example of patience can be seen in the example shown in Image 49. The play starts with the left centerback Antonio Rüdiger (2) winning the aerial duel and playing the ball to the left midfielder Jorginho (5).

Image 50

As Jorginho (5) receives the ball, we can see in Image 50 how the opponent Manchester United only has three players in the first line of pressure and the second line isn't visible until the midfield line. That is to say: they are a withdrawn team and will be difficult to surprise in transition.

Image 51

That's why Jorginho chooses to pass back to the centerback he is facing, calming the game down and providing the necessary mettle needed for the team to reorganize and build their attack from the back. In these scenarios it's very important for the two center midfielders to recognize when to go forward in a quick transition and when to be patient. In Image 51 we can see how the ball reaches the goalkeeper Édouard Mendy (16), who on this occasion chooses to play a long pass to skip the first line of pressure.

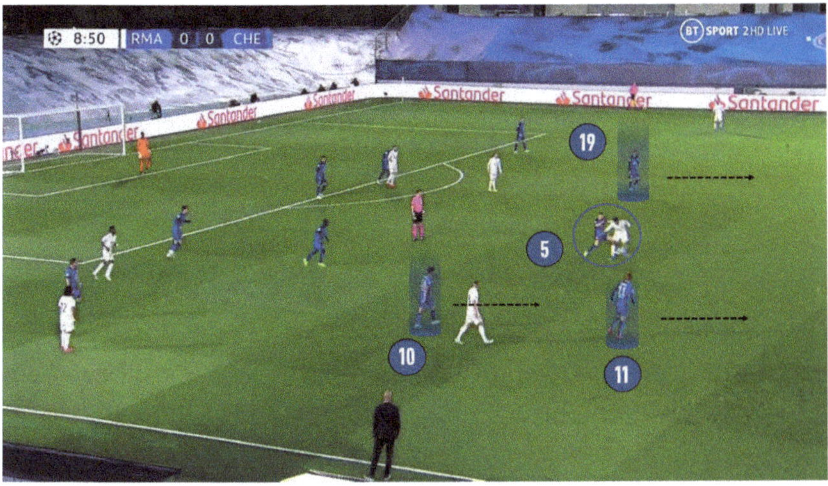

Image 52

It's in the open-field scenarios where Tuchel establishes the full potential of his teams' offensive transitions. When they start from their own half, in zone 1, it's a delight to witness their efficiency and precision. The strategy is simple: activate the two wingers and the center forward immediately after recovering the ball, limit the touches, and play vertically. In the action shown in Image 52, the left midfielder Jorginho (5) recovers the ball and the two wingers Mason Mount (19) and Christian Pulisic (10) are quickly activated, along with the center forward Timo Werner (11). The objective is to exploit the spaces left exposed by the opponent, who have seven players in their opponent's half of the field. It's a situation in which the Bavarian's teams feel very comfortable.

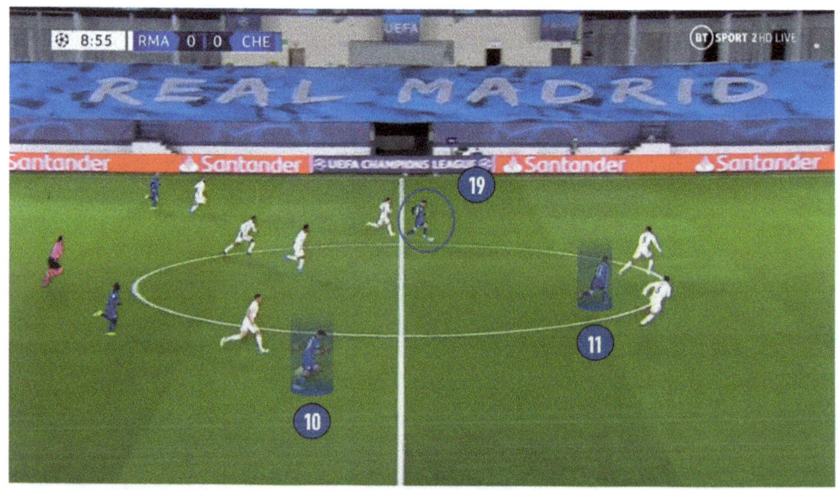

Image 53

Much of the success in this phase of the game is due to the fact that the German coach has players on the wing with ideal profiles. These essential protagonists of the offensive transitions are always fast and technically gifted. In Image 53 we see how Mount (19) takes on the responsibility for this play by running with the ball. Werner (11) plays a fundamental role, fixing the markers and positioning himself between the central defenders to generate uncertainty as to whether to step up to the Englishman or not, because doing so would free up the channel for Pulisic (10), who is accompanying the play.

Image 54

That's what allows Tuchel's team to establish itself in the opponent's penalty area in a matter of seconds, in a very advantageous one-on-one situation in which mismatches in the marking can easily occur. This is what finally happens, as reflected in Image 54. A shot by Mount (19) is blocked by the defenders, which causes disarray at the back. The ball ends up with Pulisic (10), who heads the ball on for Werner (11), who takes advantage of his marker's poor positioning to shoot without pressure. Only the great save by the goalkeeper Thibaut Courtois prevents the goal.

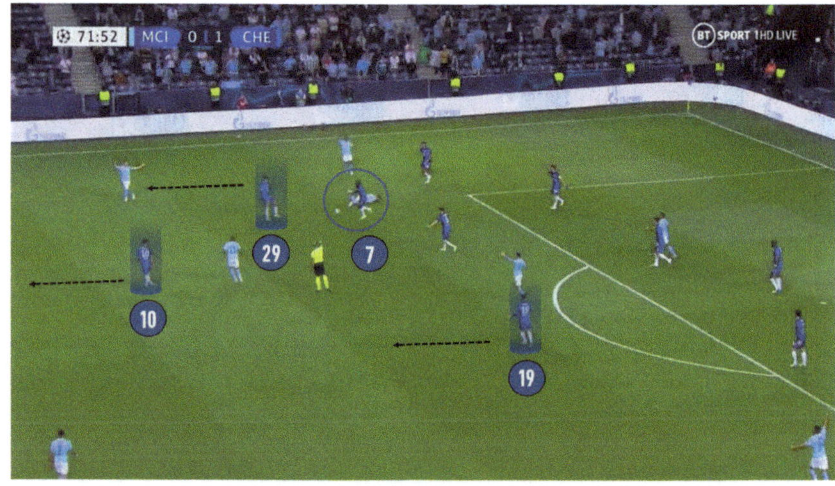

Image 55

One of Tuchel's most memorable games, due to the offensive transitions on display, is the Champions League final where his Chelsea played against and beat Pep Guardiola's Manchester City. The initial pattern (Image 55) is identical to that of the previous sequence: once the right midfielder Kanté (7) recovers the ball, the two wingers Pulisic (10) and Mount (19) and the center forward Havertz (29) are quickly activated, seeking to punish the back line of an opponent that has been drawn completely into their rival's half of the field.

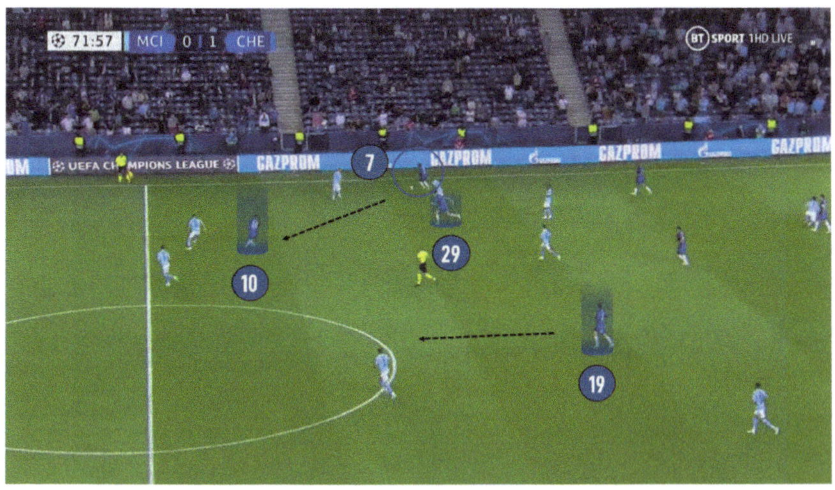

Image 56

A nuance to keep in mind during this counterattack is the positional exchange between the right winger Pulisic (10) and the center forward Havertz (29), as seen in Image 56. These situations usually occur when the center forward has a more mobile profile and is less of a target player (as in this case). Likewise, this action reflects the importance of having the midfielder who recovers the ball be the barometer to interpret which is better: to throw men forward or to build the attack patiently. In this case, Kanté (7) recognizes a favorable scenario for playing out quickly and finds Pulisic (10), who is between the centerbacks. Havertz (29) takes his first touch at speed, which allows him to advance through several meters of space to generate a one-on-one. The left winger Mason Mount (19) also follows the play from a few steps behind.

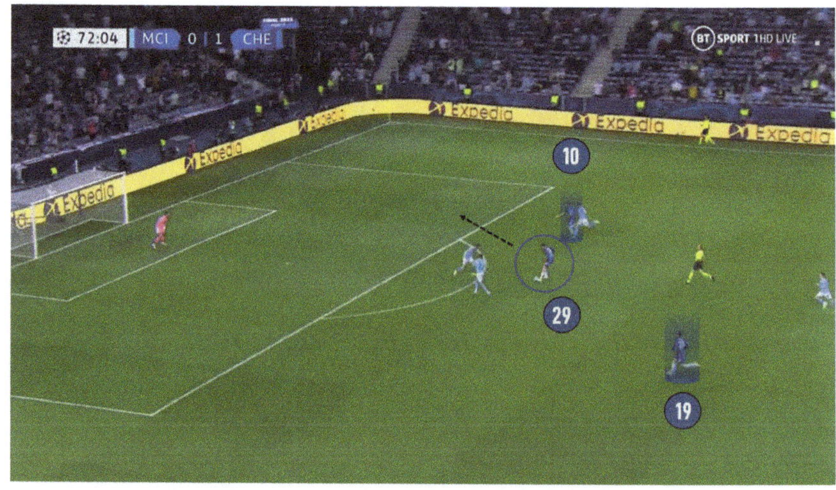

Image 57

Pulisic's (10) magnificent offload to Havertz (29) allows both players to gain the upper hand. The German bides his time in search of the right moment to filter that last pass towards the American, who only has to finish against the goalkeeper. However, this wonderful transition comes a few milimeters short of finishing with a goal. In Image 57 we see how Mount (19) stays with the action until the end, something that's characteristic of Tuchel's teams. The two wingers and the center forward must always attempt to reach finishing positions.

Image 58

In an example that follows the same pattern, Image 58 shows the ball being recovered after a clearance in zone one by the left winger Kai Havertz (29). His two teammates, the center forward Timo Werner (11) and the right winger Hakim Ziyech (22), spot the opportunity to make a quick transition and activate themselves to attack the free spaces behind the back of a team that has pushed most of their players into the opponent's half of the field.

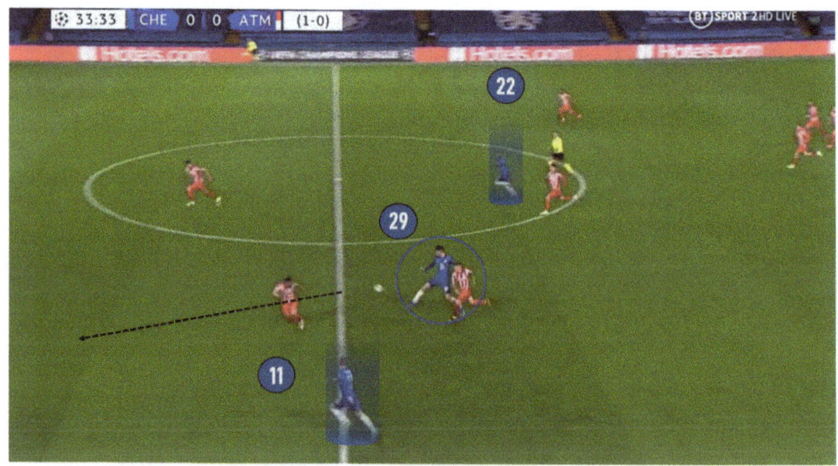

Image 59

Due to the initial positioning of the players, this time the action takes place in a wide area. As seen in Image 59, Werner (11) demands a through-pass from Havertz (29) and attacks the space behind his marker, who is unsure whether to step up to the ball or track the forward. As always, the other winger, who is Ziyech (22) in this example, accompanies the play and looks for his opportunity in the transition, which also draws the attention of the opponent.

Image 60

As the play continues, Werner (11) overcomes one of the opponents who closes him down and advances on the left side. As we can see in Image 60, the remaining centerback is unsure if he should block his opponent's path or hold his position and move back towards his goal. Somewhat belatedly, the opponent choses the first option, and the German takes advantage of this situation to send a low cross towards Ziyech (22), who recognizes the free space and attacks it at the perfect moment to finish off the chance unmarked.

This transition sums up all the common denominators: the activation of the wingers and center forward, the minimal touches as the team advances towards the opposition's goal, and the rapid driving with ball. It's what Tuchel instills in his teams and what makes them a real delight to watch. Faced with this speed of execution, rival defenses are forced into retreating very deep, making mistakes, and leaving open spaces to be exploited.

TRANSITION FROM A HIGHER BLOCK

Image 61

The behavior of Tuchel's players is quite different in situations where they recover the ball in a more advanced position. What they do in these situations is replace that blistering speed with pauses and switches of play, with the intention of exploiting the opponent's weak side. In Image 61 we can see how, thanks to good pressing, the left midfielder Mateo Kovačić (8) wins the ball practically in zone three of the pitch, but with his team in a situation of considerable structural disorder.

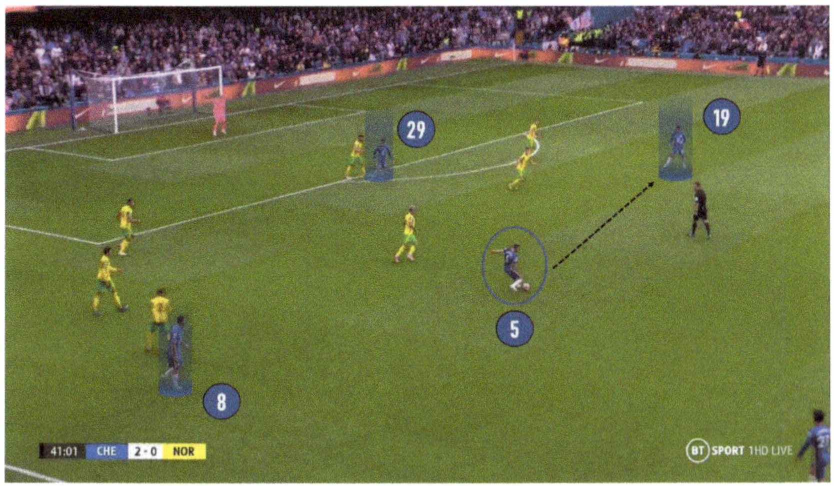

Image 62

That is why the team tries to quickly restructure itself, looking to form a recognizable ecosystem that's as similar as possible to their organized attacking mechanisms. In Image 62 we can see how Mateo Kovačić (8) immediately tries to switch play through the other midfielder to the winger on the other side. In this case, it's the right midfielder Jorginho (5) who receives the ball and finds the right winger Mason Mount (19) out wide. Image 62 also shows how the center forward Kai Havertz (29) positions himself at the edge of the penalty area in order to fix the centerbacks, a very recognizable behavior in the organized attacks of Tuchel's teams.

Image 63

By switching the action to the other side, the Bavarian's team looks to either find a superiority on the outside or take advantage of any imbalance in the opponent's defensive transition. On this occasion the second option occurs: Norwich does not shift well, and this allows the right wingback Reece James (24) to attack the interval between the centerback and the fullback, get in behind both of them, and receive a precise pass into space from Mount (19) to score a beautifully crafted goal.

Image 64

   This example demonstrates how Tuchel's teams combine three behaviors: the pause, block restructuring, and the switch of play. In Image 64 we can see how both teams have a large number of players on the left side of the field after the German's team recovers the ball in zone two. The barometer of the group, the left midfielder Mateo Kovačić (17) recognizes this and imposes the pause required to enable the other two behaviors: organizing the offensive structure and attacking the opponent's weak side.

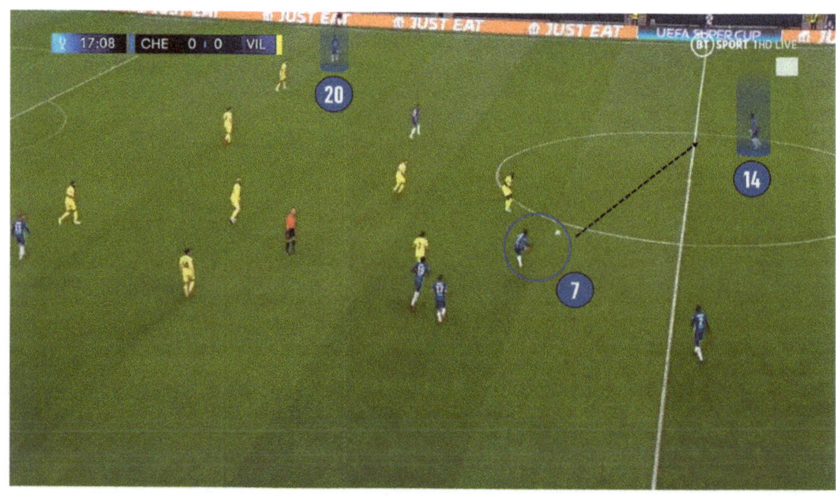

Image 65

In just a few seconds, Tuchel's team is forcing the opponent to shift. They do this with several backwards passes, the ones necessary to organize their block and guide the play to the other side of the field. In Image 65 we see how the midfielders provide support. In this case it's the right midfielder N'Golo Kanté (7) who is responsible for expanding the play through the right back Trevoh Chalobah (14), whose support offers the width necessary to quickly deliver the ball to the other side of the field. When the Englishman receives the ball, we see that he has a clean passing line to the right back Callum Hudson-Odoi (20), who is in a position to engage in a one-on-one or a two-on-one if the nearby winger joins in. This allows the team to find the kind of superiority on the outside that Tuchel likes so much.

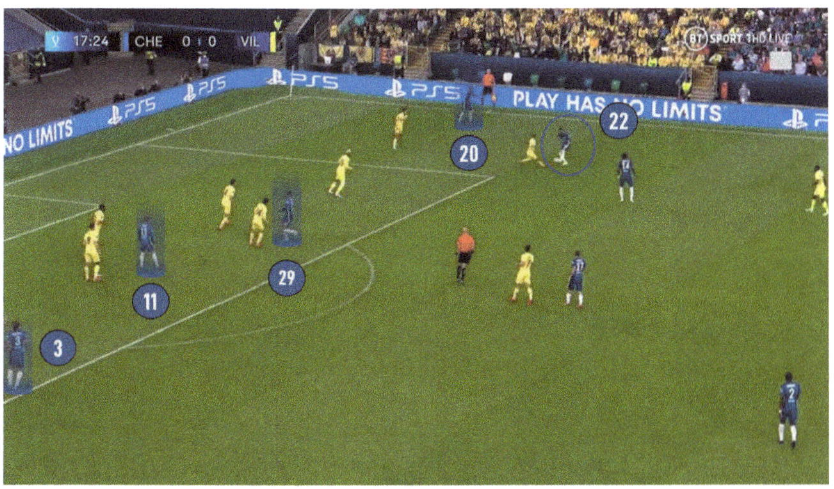

Image 66

After several combinations, the play finally ends up where the Bavarian coach makes his teams feel the most comfortable: looking for superiorities in the outer channels. In this case, as we can see in Image 66, the superiority emerges from the wingback Hudson-Odoi (20) and the right winger Hakim Ziyech (22). During the process that has brought the play to this situation, the team has had time to settle into the opposition's penalty area in a very recognizable way, with the winger-center forward-wingback structure (from right to left) that we have previously analyzed. With the left winger Kai Havertz (29) operating freely in the near post area, the center forward Timo Werner (11) fixing a central defender, and the left wingback Marcos Alonso (3) appearing at the far post, a rational occupation of space has been achieved.

In conclusion, Tuchel's teams have two very different ways of behaving after winning the ball, depending on where they do it. If they recover the ball with their block farther back, they try to reach the opposing goal as quickly as possible. If they win the ball with their block in an advanced position, they put more emphasis on playing comfortably and taking advantage of their superiorities to look for a good finishing opportunity.

ORGANIZED DEFENSE

Basic Principles:

Defensive positional formations.

When playing at home or against a theoretically inferior opponent, Tuchel's teams press the buildout with a high block in a 1-3-4-2-1. Other options include the 1-4-3-3 and the 1-4-2-3-1.

Alternative defensive positional formations.

Against a theoretically superior opponent or when playing to preserve a favorable result, he opts for a medium-low block with the lines playing very close together in a 1-5-3-2. Other options include the 1-4-3-3 and the 1-4-2-3-1.

Behavior of the team when defending against the buildout or progression of the opponent.

The German coach's teams always defend with the idea of protecting the inside and forcing the opponent to seek progression on the outside, where they can deploy their most effective defensive mechanisms.

Behavior of the team when defending the opponent in the finishing phase.

They defend by accumulating players inside the penalty area, with well-positioned central defenders near the penalty spot and with the wingbacks and at least one midfielder helping out.

Defensive strength is a recognized feature of Tuchel's teams. In the organized defensive phase we can see the most adaptive facet of the German coach's game. Since he is not married to any specific formation, everything depends on the opponent, the context of the match, and the score at that moment. Depending on what suits his team best, the team's defensive behavior can even vary within the same match.

The Bavarian's teams can be described as using a mix of defensive concepts, with the ability to press in a medium-high block in order to aggressively recover the ball. On the other hand, they also feel very comfortable dropping back into a low block, with their lines close together. Their greatest strength comes from this chameleon-like adaptability, since they know how to handle themselves in every possible scenario.

Next, in Images 67, 68, and 69, we will see the three main defensive behaviors of Tuchel's teams.

1-5-3-2 in a low block

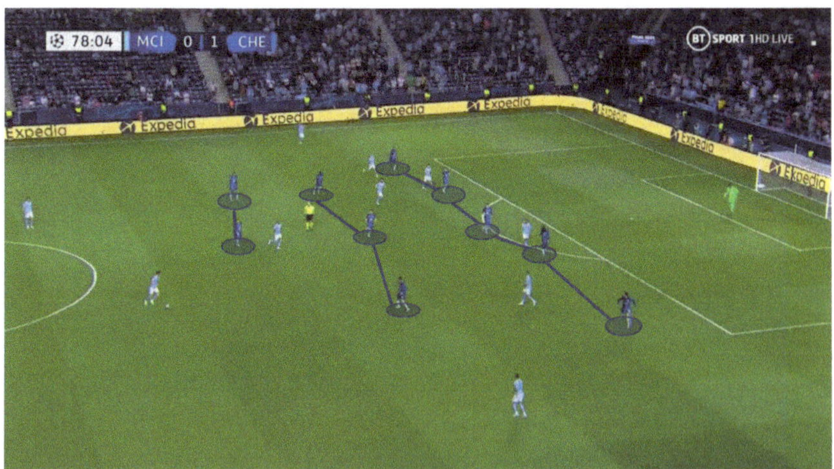

Image 67

1-5-3-2 in a medium block

Image 68

1-3-4-2-1 in a high block

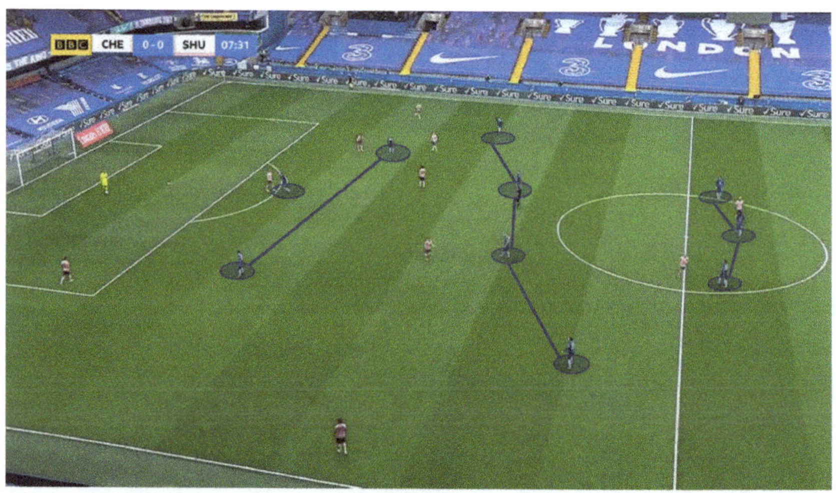

Image 69

Within these structures there are automatisms that Tuchel establishes in his defensive system when defending both the opponent's buildout and progression and their finishing.

DEFENDING THE BUILDOUT AND PROGRESSION OF THE OPPONENT

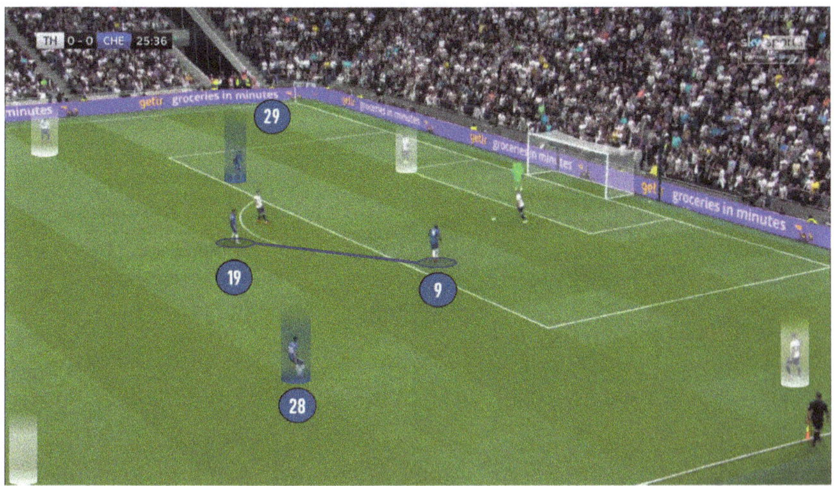

Image 70

There are two basic concepts when Tuchel's teams go to press the opponent's buildout: cover the progression from the inside, forcing the opponent to play outside or go long, and using the winger and the wingback in the intermediate spaces on the opposite side (who step up to position themselves between the opponent's fullback and winger). In Image 70 we see how the right winger Mason Mount (19) and the center forward Romelu Lukaku (9) block the interior channels. Additionally, the left winger Kai Havertz (29) and the right wingback Cesar Azpilicueta (28) position themselves between two opponents to quickly activate themselves if there is a pass to either of these two players.

Due to this good defensive work, the opponent is forced to play long.

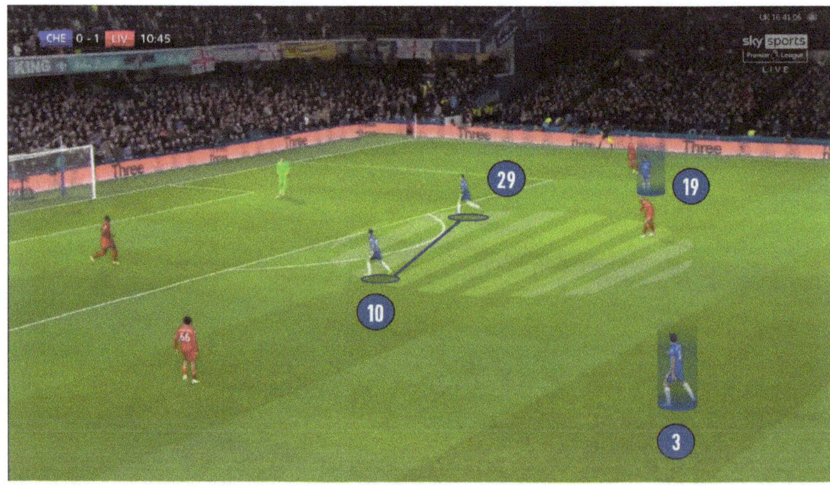

Image 71

We see the same arrangement in Image 71. The center forward Kai Havertz (29) is positioned alongside the left winger Christian Pulisic (10) to make inside passes impossible. On the flanks, the right winger Mason Mount (19) and the left wingback Marcos Alonso (3) are positioned in intermediate positions. Once again they force the opponent, in this case Jürgen Klopp's Liverpool, to play long in the buildout.

Image 72

Image 72 shows the same setup, with the team stepping up to pressure in a high block. The center forward Timo Werner (11) and the right winger Hakim Ziyech (22) prevent the inside pass, while the left winger Mason Mount (19) and the right wingback Cesar Azpilicueta (28) are positioned in intermediate positions between the fullbacks and opposing wingers on each flank, in order to quickly activate themselves to oppose a pass in any direction. This arrangement from Tuchel's group once again forces a long clearance.

Image 73

Once the German's opponent has managed to overcome the first line of pressure, his team drops down to wait in a medium or low block. The Bavarian attaches great importance to blocking inside passes and trying to smother the opponent on the wings, defending positionally in a diamond. The structure is always the same, comprising the winger, the wingback, the midfielder and the centerback from that side. In Image 73 we can see this clearly: the structure is made up of the left winger Christian Pulisic (10), the left wingback Ben Chilwell (21), the left midfielder N'Golo Kanté (7) - who shifts to that side - , and the left centerback Antonio Rüdiger (2).

This makes it impossible for the opponent to make any connection to the inside and traps any player who enters this perfectly structured cage.

Image 74

Tuchel has made it so that his teams are tremendously difficult to attack through the central areas of the field when they are in the organized defensive phase. On many occasions their opponents are limited to lateral crosses, actions that the German's teams are good at defending. Image 74 again reflects this diamond defense created by the left winger Mason Mount (19), the left back Ben Chilwell (21), the left midfielder N'Golo Kanté (7), and the left centerback Antonio Rudiger (2). This situation forces the opponent to drop the ball back and restart play, because they are unable to find passing lines that will allow them to progress.

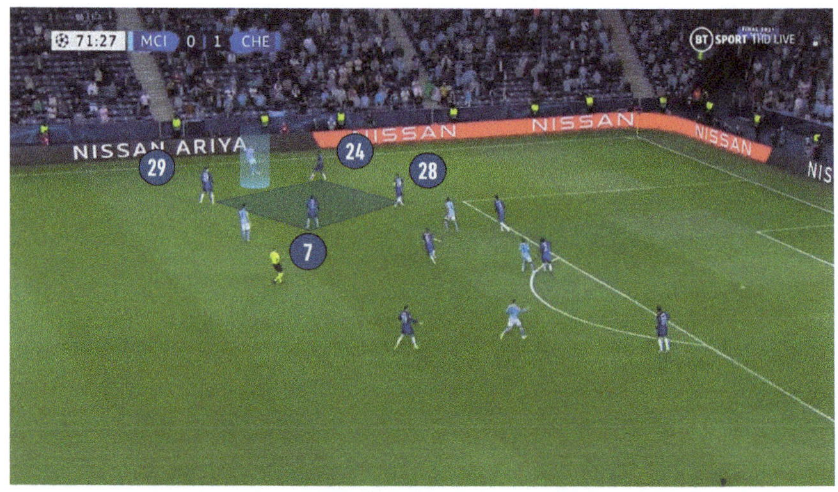

Image 75

Image 76

These two images are very interesting for contextualizing the zonal defending in a diamond shape. The fact that only ten seconds pass between one situation and the next reflects how much the German coach trains these actions.

In Image 75 we see how Chelsea manages to isolate Pep Guardiola's Manchester City and makes it difficult for them to play through the interior channels, something Tuchel's team feels very comfortable doing, during the final minutes of the Champions League final. In the first moment, the diamond structure is formed by the right winger Kai Havertz (29), the right back Reece James (24), the right midfielder, N'Golo Kanté (7), and the right centerback César Azpilicueta (28).

As the action continues, City is unable to connect inside and decides to direct play to the other side. But after switching play they finds themselves facing the same defensive structure, as shown in Image 76. This time the structure is made up of the left winger Mason Mount (19), the left back Ben Chilwell (21), the left midfielder Mateo Kovačić (17), and the left centerback Antonio Rüdiger (2).

The defensive automatisms that Tuchel achieves with his teams are very focused and stable, which makes them one of the most reliable teams in the world in these situations.

DEFENDING OPPONENTS IN THE FINISHING PHASE

Image 77

Tuchel's teams have a very well-organized defensive structure in the opponent's finishing zone. They choose to accumulate men inside the penalty area in order to cover crosses and to deny the opponent good finishing opportunities.

As we can see in Image 77, the main axis is made up of the centerbacks who are rationally distributed near the penalty spot. Normally one of the wingbacks attempts to block the opponent's delivery, as the right-sided César Azpilicueta (28) does in this example. Meanwhile, the opposite wingback will narrow his position so that he can defend any ball that might reach the area at the far post, as we can see Marcos Alonso (3) do in this image.

Finally, the midfielders play very interesting roles: one of them positions themselves in the gap between the centerback and the winger to try to block any inside passing options or to block short crosses to the near post. In Image 77 we can see how the right midfielder N'Golo Kanté (7) is perfectly positioned to do this.

Image 78

In the action shown in Image 78 we can see another clear example of this structure, with the centerbacks again distributed in an orderly manner within the penalty area. In addition, the left wingback Marcos Alonso (3) comes out to try to block the opponent's cross and the right wingback Reece James (24) narrows his position and adjusts his depth to put himself closer to the other defenders near the far post. One nuance of this play is the positioning of the right midfielder N'Golo Kanté (7), who is a little higher up than in the previous situation to cover the inside passing options towards the edge of the area.

Image 79

During situations in which the block defends very low, there are small variations in the positioning to try to cover more spaces in the penalty area and ensure the greatest possible protection. In Image 79 we see Tuchel's team defending against an opponent who, with the intention of equalizing, accumulates a lot of players in the finishing zone. That is why the Bavarian coach prefers to adjust the structure in these situations, with both wingbacks inside the area. This means that one of the wingers must attempt to prevent the cross.

We can see how the left wingback Ben Chilwell (21) positions himself in an area previously occupied by a midfielder. The wingback on the opposite side, in this case César Azpilicueta (28), still closes in at the far post. As always, the central defenders maintain their well-structured positioning in the penalty area. One of the midfielders, in this example the right midfielder N'Golo Kanté (7), is positioned at the top of the penalty area to deal with any clearances or rebounds.

DEFENSIVE TRANSITION

Basic principles:

Centerbacks delaying the attack

When Tuchel's teams attack in a high block, there are many situations where the centerbacks find themselves with a great deal of space behind them. This is space that they must manage, delaying the opponent's attack when the ball is lost to allow the rest of the players time to recover their defensive structure.

The physical demands on the wingbacks

The German coach places a very demanding physical load on these players. This is because they must always be active in the attack and also drop back quickly to their defensive positions, responsibilities that require them to constantly get up and down the pitch.

Directing the ball towards the wings to press

Tuchel is obsessed with protecting the inside of the field when defending. Faced with a loss of possession with their block at a medium-low height, his teams focus their pressure to push the opponent's play to the wings, where they feel the most comfortable defending and pressing.

As one would expect, Tuchel also creates very clear and specific patterns for his team's defensive transitions. Playing with two wingbacks who are so active in the attacking zone during the offensive phase of the game has its risks, which is why retreating after a loss or possession when the team is in the opponent's half of the field is very important. That's why the centerbacks must know how to delay counterattacks in order to give their teammates time to restructure themselves defensively, especially the wingbacks who are such important assets for Tuchel's teams in moments without the ball.

In situations where the loss of possession occurs when the block is in a less advanced position, the German coach initiates pressure that is oriented towards the outside. This is because these are the areas where their players feel most comfortable defending, and where they know how to pressure and trap their opponent in order to recover the ball.

CENTERBACKS DELAYING THE ATTACK AND WINGBACKS DROPPING BACK

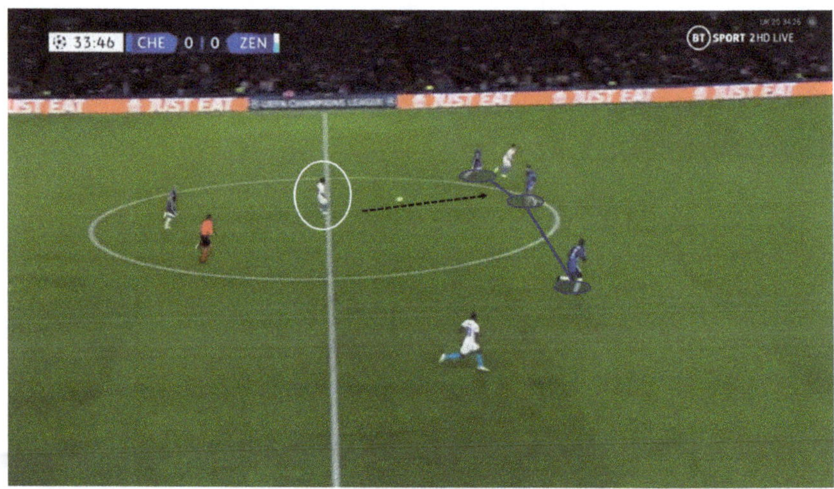

Image 80

In Image 80 we can see a clear example of this: the opponent carries out a quick offensive transition and Tuchel's team is exposed in a three-on-three situation, with lots of space behind their centerbacks. That's why the defenders must perfectly manage these actions and execute these automatisms.

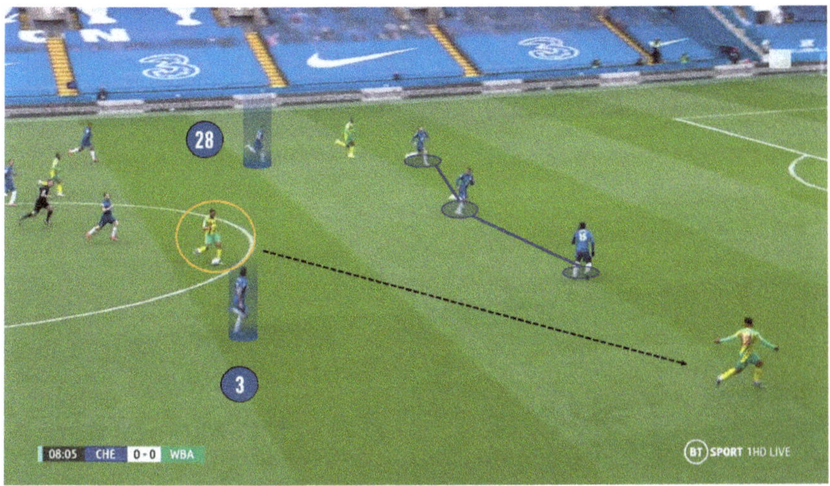

Image 81

In this counterattacking action it's important to focus on the height of the wingbacks. As we can see in Image 81, the three retreating players must delay the attack to give the two wingbacks time to drop back and help, so that there will be no opportunity for the opponent to go one-on-one with the goalkeeper. The left wingback Marcos Alonso (3) and the right wingback César Azpilicueta (28) have a lot of ground to cover.

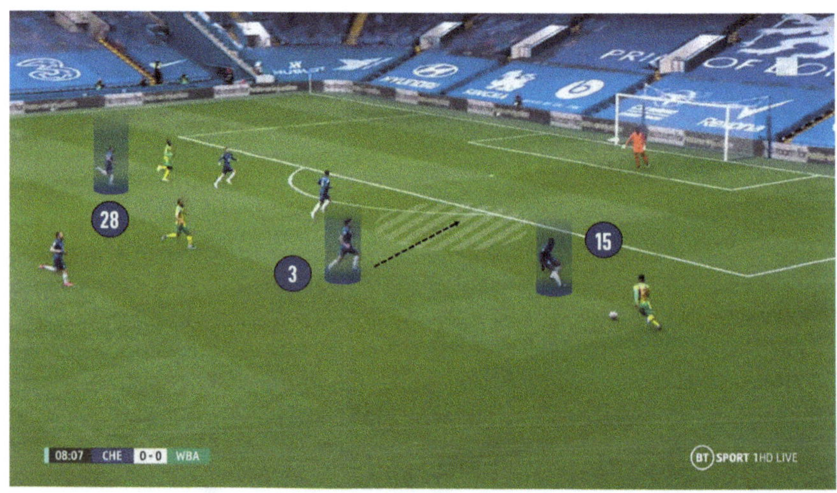

Image 82

As soon as the wingback Marcos Alonso (3) arrives (in Image 82), the left centerback Kurt Zouma (15) goes out to confront the opposing attacker and prevent the cross. He can do this because he knows that the Spaniard will occupy the space that he just vacated, in a very elaborate automatism that is repeated regularly in the defensive transitions of Tuchel's teams, where players know they will have to run a long way back towards their own goal. On the other side of the field we see how the right wingback César Azpilicueta (28) has time to drop back to defend any delivery towards that area.

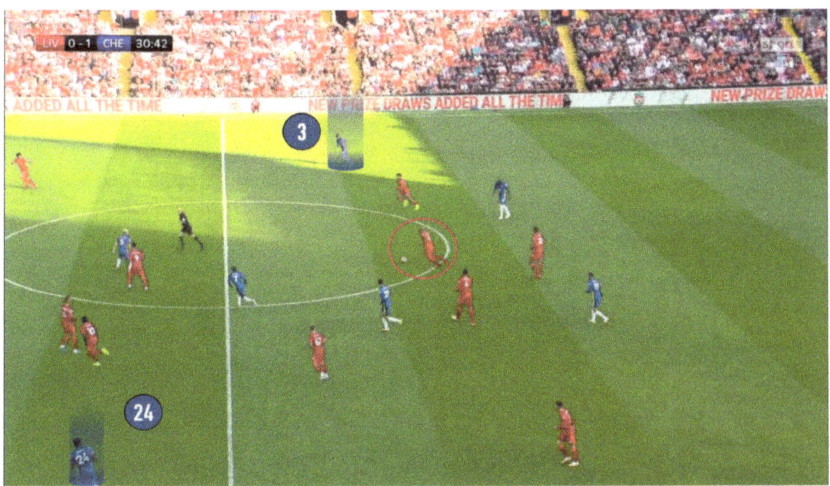

Image 83

The action shown in Image 83 demands another intense recovery from Marcos Alonso (3) and Reece James (24), the left and right wingbacks respectively, due to a loss of possession in the midfield area. These efforts are undertaken constantly throughout the game, and the physical capacity of the players in these positions must be high enough to meet the German coach's demands. This is the most specific responsibility in his system of play.

Image 84

Just as in the previous situation, in Image 84 we can see how the left centerback Antonio Rüdiger (2) goes out to meet Mohamed Salah while Alonso (3) moves quickly to momentarily occupy the German's position. In this way, he rebalances his team's defensive positioning. On the other side, Reece James (24) narrows his position and takes advantage of the good delaying action by the other defenders, arriving at the right moment and minimizing the opponent's chances of finishing.

DIRECTING THE BALL TOWARDS THE WINGS TO PRESS

Image 85

In situations where Tuchel's teams lose the ball with their block less advanced, the strategy is clear: quickly cover any inside passing lines and cede the wing to the opponent. It's in these wide areas that the team will then quickly activate the press and try to recover the ball as quickly as possible. In Image 85 we see how the German coach's players make it impossible for the opposing centerback to connect any inside passes, which forces Porto to progress on the outside.

Image 86

As we have previously seen in the organized defense phase, Tuchel's teams feel very comfortable defending on the outside while restricting the inside spaces. In defensive transitions, the German coach seeks to produce very similar situations in order to recover the ball as soon as possible, and also to buy time for the team to comfortably recover their defensive positions. Once the Porto centerback connects with the winger who has dropped down to receive the ball, pressure is initiated with the objective of taking the ball away as quickly as possible. As we can see in Image 85, a very favorable three-on-one on has been created on the wing.

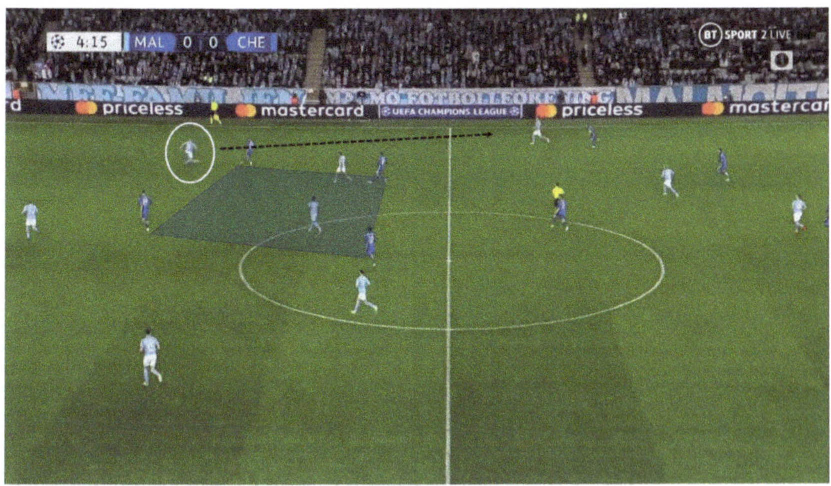

Image 87

The situation we see in Image 87 follows the same pattern: after losing the ball in a lower block, Tuchel's team uses their most advanced players to close the inside spaces so that the opponent Malmö only has the option to progress on the outside.

Image 88

Once the Malmö winger receives the ball (Image 88), this once again triggers an intense activation of Tuchel's nearest defenders. And once again, a three-on-one situation has been created on the wing, blocking any option for the attacker to pass to either the centerback or any of the supporting midfielders. This is an ideal situation for the Bavarian coach's teams, as they can orient their press to the wing and pressure the player on the ball.

Image 89

In the situation shown in Image 89, we can see a somewhat different situation, but one that has the same objective and mechanisms and produces the same result: a press after losing the ball that only allows their rival the option of progressing on the outside. The key figure is the right winger Hakim Ziyech (22), who quickly moves to position himself in the passing line between the opponent's winger and central defender after the ball is lost, which prevents any passes inside. This forces the opponent to delay playing the ball and prevents a quick transition.

Image 90

The team presses in a way that forces the ball back to the opposing goalkeeper, and once again they entice him to build out through the wing. In Image 90 we see how the first line of pressure from Tuchel's team moves into the opponent's penalty area and blocks any buildout on the inside, forcing the goalkeeper to either pass to the fullback (in a possibly compromised situation) or play long. He chooses the second option, which favors a rapid recovery by the Bavarian coach's team.

SET PLAYS

Basic Principles:

Offensive set plays

Tuchel's teams have mastered a wide range of actions with an infinite number of positioning schemes, highlighted by the use of screens and dragging movements to escaper marking and generate a clean shot at goal by a player entering from the second line. His teams are also very good at exploiting second balls.

Defensive set plays

In these situations, the German coach always tends to use mixed defending, with some players occupying spaces and others marking man-to-man. In general, his best players in the air do not mark and are used to cover the areas that are most vunerable to an opponent's delivery.

Offensive set plays

Tuchel's catalog of offensive set pieces is extensive. We will see the most recognizable themes, such as the screens and dragging movements, repeated in the vast majority of these actions (especially on corners).

Image 91

The sequence that begins in Image 91 shows how two players, in this case Thiago Silva (6) and Antonio Rüdiger (2), can benefit from the previous movements of their teammates in order to arrive from the second line with a shooting opportunity. At the near post, Christian Pulisic (10) feints an approach to receive the ball short, prompting Luka Modrić to follow him and leave that area free. César Azpilicueta (28) executes another dragging movement towards the goalkeeper's box, also forcing his marker to follow him. In addition, Kai Havertz (29) is in the target zone, setting a screen to help the shooters reach that space without marking.

Image 92

As the corner is taken, all these movements contribute to freeing up space in the area around the penalty spot. This is the perfect place for Thiago Silva (6) to execute an unmarked header. Image 92 is also useful for highlighting the previously mentioned concepts: the dragging movements of Pulisic (10) and Azpilicueta (28) and the screen by Havertz (29). It's a perfectly rehearsed play that almost ends in a goal.

Image 93

Image 93 shows some additional general aspects from Tuchel's set play notebook, related to the behavior of the team as a block during offensive corner kicks. First, we see an initial group of players who set screens that the second group (the shooters) can make use of when they reach the goal. Next, we can see the value that the German coach gives to controlling the top of the penalty area, where he always places players who strike the ball well for a possible shot or a second ball played back into the box.

Image 94

Image 94 shows another good maneuver using screens, which Kai Havertz (29) and Ruben Loftus-Cheek (12) execute for the benefit of Thiago Silva (6). The Brazilian attacks the area at the near post from the second line, looking to finish the play.

Image 95

Before the corner is taken (Image 95), Thiago Silva (6) already knows which area he must attack and takes full advantage of his teammates' screens to shoot while completely unmarked. In another magnificent action rehearsed by the German coach, a goal is only prevented by the defender's goal line clearance.

Image 96

As we have seen, Tuchel pays attention to every detail and leaves nothing to chance. This is especially true of set play situations. He always places great importance on having players with good shooting ability occupying the clearance zone at the edge of the penalty area. In Image 95 we see an example of how Mateo Kovačić (8) and Mason Mount (19) wait alertly to react to any second ball.

Image 97

In Image 97 we see how the ball lands in the area where the players with the best striking ability tend to be. Mateo Kovačić (8) is waiting for his opportunity, and the Croatian manages to adjust his body and crack a shot into the top corner, a difficult and beautifully crafted strike.

DEFENSIVE SET PLAYS

A major strength of the teams that Tuchel builds is that they are very difficult to hurt on set pieces. Now, we will analyze their basic positioning when defending against these types of plays.

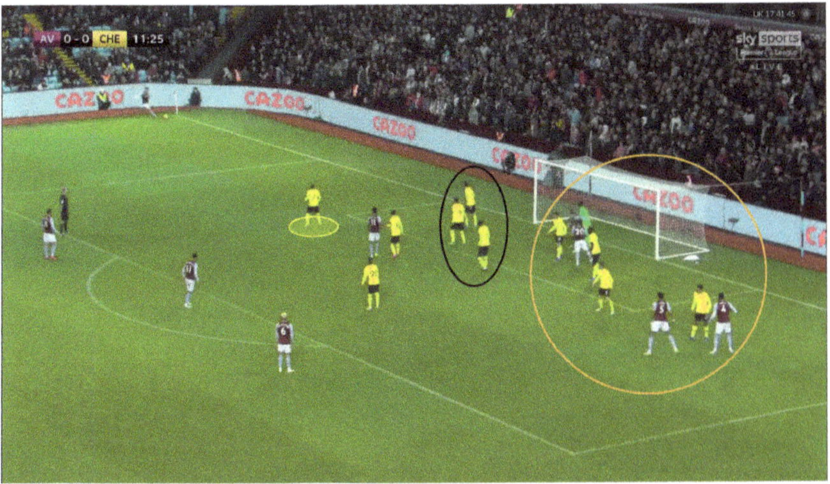

Image 98

When defending corners (Image 98), the team opts for a mixed marking system. A first block of players covers an area with one player at the near post and two with strong aerial ability (normally, two centerbacks) at the front of the goalkeeper's box. But the second group marks man-to-man, which in this case requires them to start at the far post. In addition, there is always a player guarding against a possible short corner.

Image 99

In Image 99 we observe the same mixed defending, starting with an identical first block of players (one covering the near post and two defending zonally in the goalkeeper's box). In this situation, the second group is positioned near the penalty spot, making man-to-man. In every situation, their positioning is greatly dependent on the distribution of the opponent's potential finishers. There is also one player disconnected from the block, watching for a short delivery.

Image 100

As Image 100 shows, another variant that Tuchel teams typically use to defend corner kicks consists of placing three players marking zonally just in front of the goalkeeper, placing another two somewhat further forward who also mark zonally, and then leaving the remaining block of players to mark man-to-man. As before, one player is disconnected from the block to guard against a short corner. With this mixed strategy, the German coach shows that his objective in these situations is to occupy the vulnerable areas in a perfectly uniform way, with the individual markers adding extra protection. This leaves the opponent very few options to spring a surprise.

Image 101

This last example shows the same distribution in a mixed defense: three players marking zonally in the space near the goalkeeper, two additional zonal defenders a bit further forward, and the block of man-markers. As in all these actions, there is a player protecting against a short delivery.

TUCHEL: THE PRESENT AND THE FUTURE OF GERMAN COACHING

The evolution that German coaching has experienced in recent years and the number of coaches they have exported for the highest level of the game incredible. Without a doubt, Thomas Tuchel is one of their most notable examples on the international scene today, along with Julian Nagelsmann.

Having analyzed his career, his evolution, and how he develops his teams, the Bavarian's career path poses a very good question for his future on the sidelines: will he establish the 1-3-4-2-1, the formation he has employed the most at Chelsea, at any of his future destinations, or will he continue to adapt to whatever prevailing ecosystem he finds himself in? His current favorite system requires very specific demands and a high level of physical capacity from players in certain positions, something that not every squad can provide. But without a doubt, this is the system that has provided him with his most important successes so far, and which has allowed him to express his own unique and distinctive playing philosophy.

What is clear is that his experiences and achievements up to this point will continue to secure him a place on the sidelines of the world's top clubs for years to come. He is both the present and the future of German coaching.

TRAINING ACTIVITIES

RONDO WITH WIDE PLAYERS

OBJECTIVES OF THE ACTIVITY

- Accumulating passes.
- Making decisions in superiority.
- Rational occupation of spaces.
- Defensive shifting.
- Switching play.
- Preventing interior passes.

Nº Of players	Phase	Duration
5v3	INITIAL	10 MIN

RULES

- In the space marked out in the illustration plus the free exterior spaces, the objective is to create superiorities in the wide areas.
- The defending players must occupy the two interior spaces.
- The attackers should use the interior player to help switch the ball from one zone to the other.
- Optional: Impose touch limits. Award points after a certain number of consecutive passes.

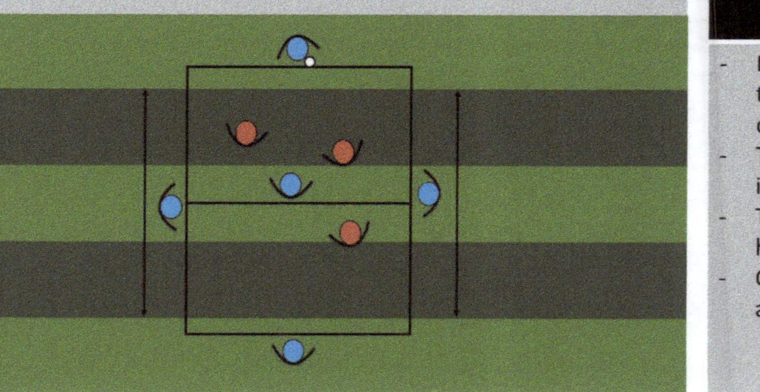

RONDO + 2v1 FINISHING

OBJECTIVES OF THE ACTIVITY

- Finishing in superiority.
- Pressing after losing the ball.
- Defensive shifting.
- Accumulating passes.

Nº Of players	Phase	Duration
4v3	INITIAL	10 MIN

RULES

- In the space marked out in the illustration, play a 3v1 rondo.
- After winning the ball, the blue player looks to connect with the two teammates waiting in the larger area.
- Blue attempts to finish in a 2v1, using as few touches as possible, .
- Optional: Use a large goal with a goalkeeper. Allow the player defending in the rondo to participate in the finishing phase.

POSSESSION IN SUPERIORITY: 4v4+4 NEUTRALS

OBJECTIVES OF THE ACTIVITY

- Decisions in superiority.
- Accumulating passes.
- Closing the interior spaces.
- Support on the outside.
- Pressing after losing the ball.
- Switching play.
- Wingbacks in support.
- Finishing.

Nº Of players	Phase	Duration
4v4+4N	MAIN	15-20 MIN

RULES

- In the space marked out in the illustration plus the free exterior spaces, the objective is to create superiorities with both the interior and exterior neutral players.
- Require a minimum number of passes before finishing in the mini-goals.
- Optional: Use two big goals instead of the mini-goals in order to incorporate the goalkeepers.

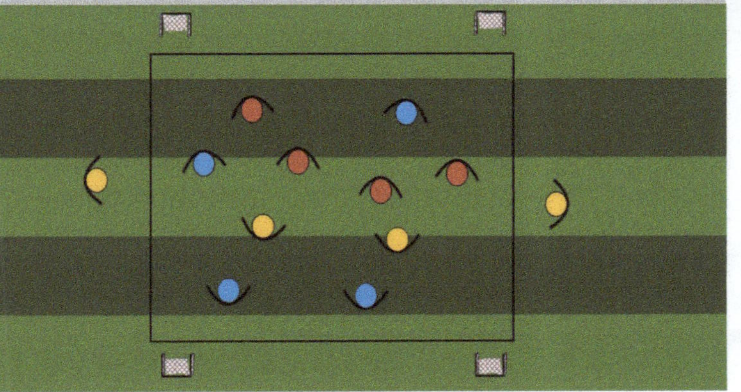

BUILDOUT AND PROGRESSION: 3 CENTERBACKS + 2 WINGBACKS

OBJECTIVES OF THE ACTIVITY

- Superiorities on the outside.
- Pressing after losing the ball.
- Rational occupation of spaces.
- Defensive shifting.
- Building out of the back.
- Wingbacks in support.

Nº Of players	Phase	Duration
8v8+2N	FINAL	15-20 MIN

RULES

- In the space marked out in the illustration plus the free exterior spaces, the objective is to create superiorities out wide with the exterior neutral players.
- The players in the interior spaces are confined to their respective zones and must look for superiorities with the neutrals.
- Teams may only finish after the ball has passed through all three zones.

SMALL SIDED GAME: 3v3 + 2 NEUTRALS

OBJECTIVES OF THE ACTIVITY

- Superiorities on the outside.
- Defensive shifting.
- Finishing in transition.
- Defending crosses.
- Switching play.

Nº Of players	Phase	Duration
3v3+2N	MAIN	15 MIN

RULES

- In the space marked out in the illustration plus the free exterior spaces, the objective is to create superiorities out wide with the exterior neutral players.
- Both neutrals must be involved before finishing.
- Optional: Require a minimum number of passes before finishing. Require only one of the neutrals to be involved before finishing.

TRANSITIONS: 3v2/4v3

OBJECTIVES OF THE ACTIVITY

- Offensive and defensive transitions.
- Defensive shifting.
- Finishing in transition.
- Defending crosses.

Nº Of players	Phase	Duration
3v2/4v3	MAIN	15 MIN

RULES

- In the space marked out in the illustration, the red team carries out a 3v2 as quickly as possible.
- After finishing the action, the two exterior blue players join in to create a 4v3 transition in the other direction.
- Optional: Use mini-goals if goalkeepers are not available.

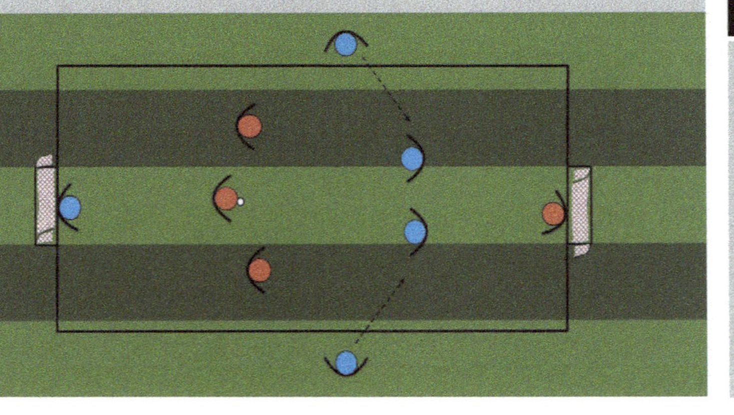

TRANSITIONS: 1v1

OBJECTIVES OF THE ACTIVITY

- Offensive and defensive transitions.
- 1 vs 1.
- Finishing.
- Speed of reactions.

Nº Of players	Phase	Duration
1v1	MAIN	10 MIN

RULES

- In the space marked out in the illustration, the objective is to train finishing and defensive transitions.
- Blue attacks the red defender 1v1, and immediately after finishing the action positions themselves to defend a new 1v1 against red, who dribbles into the playing area.
- Optional: Use small goals if goalkeepers are not available.

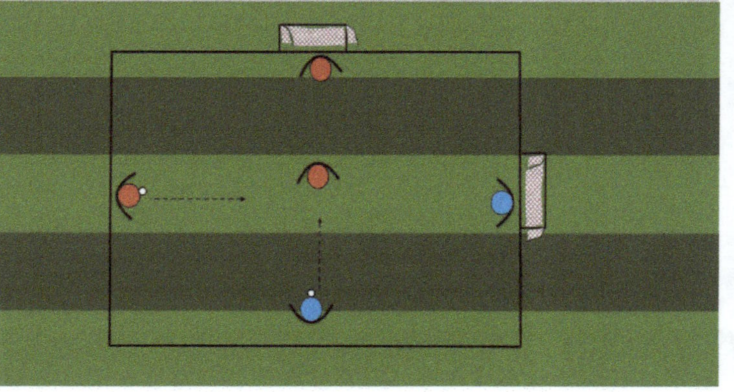

EXERCISE BEFORE THE CHAMPIONS LEAGUE FINAL 1

OBJECTIVES OF THE ACTIVITY

- Superiorities on the outside.
- Defensive shifting.
- Pressing after losing the ball.
- Rational occupation of spaces.

Nº Of players	Phase	Duration
7v7+8N	MAIN	30 MIN

RULES

- In a diamond-shaped area as shown in the illustration plus the exterior spaces, the objective is to create superiorities on the outside with the help of the neutral players.
- Look to accumulate passes, with a penalty for the defending team if a certain number of consecutive passes is reached.
- Optional: Play with fewer players in the interior area. Touch limits for the neutrals.

EXERCISE BEFORE THE CHAMPIONS LEAGUE FINAL 2

OBJECTIVES OF THE ACTIVITY

- Superiorities on the outside.
- Finishing.
- Quick transitions.
- Rational occupation of spaces.

Nº Of players	Phase	Duration
7v7+9N	MAIN	30 MIN

RULES

- In a reduced playing area as shown in the illustration plus the exterior spaces, the objective is to create superiorities on the outside with the help of the neutral players.
- Treat the activity as a game in terms of rapid ball circulation and how space is interpreted.
- Optional: Goals count double if the neutrals next to the goal are involved in the play. Require a minimum number of passes before a goal can be scored.

3 CENTERBACKS IN THE FINISHING ZONE

OBJECTIVES OF THE ACTIVITY

- Defensive positioning of the centerbacks.
- Aerial play.
- Incorporating the wingbacks.
- Crosses and finishing.

Nº Of players	Phase	Duration
4v3	FINAL	15 MIN

RULES

- In the space marked out in the illustration, look to finish in a 4v3 situation.
- The centerbacks may not leave the triangle to intercept the ball, and must work on making defensive adjustments.
- Optional: Finish within a maximum number of passes. Attackers can only finish from inside the triangle. Require the wingback on the far side to attack from inside the triangle.

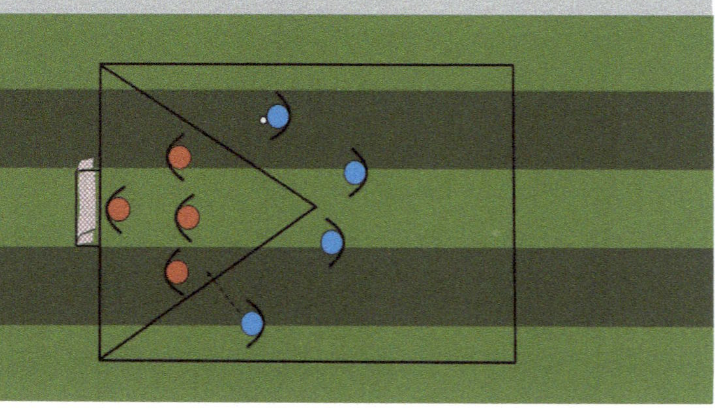

ABOUT THE AUTHOR

Born in the city of Barcelona (Spain), Carlos Domínguez is a specialist in tactical analysis. He completed the University Expert in Smart Data applied to the world of football certification and has Masters focused on Scouting (UCAM). He also has a background in data visualization, heavily focused on reporting to coaching staffs and clubs. He is currently responsible for the performance analyst and scouting duties for the Juvenil A team at EE Guineueta (Barcelona).